I Dreamt I Dwelt in Marble Halls

A play by
Ade Morris

Based on a short story by
Bryan Gallagher

Samuel French — London
www.samuelfrench-london.co.uk

I DREAMT I DWELT IN
MARBLE HALLS

First produced at The Watermill Theatre, Newbury in
March 2002 with the following cast of characters:

The Man/George   Shaun Hennesey
Madelyn/Maddy   Ann Marcusson
Daniel/Liam   Matthew Morrison

Directed by Ade Morris
Designed by Libby Watson
Lighting designed by Lawrence T. Doyle

It was revived by The Watermill Theatre, Newbury in
March 2006 with the following cast of characters:

The Man/George   Shaun Hennesey
Madelyn/Maddy   Katarina Olsson
Daniel/Liam   Justin McCarron

Directed by Ade Morris
Designed by Libby Watson
Lighting designed by Lawrence T. Doyle

CHARACTERS

Madelyn Ingram, a great beauty; mid twenties
"Mad" Maddy, an older Madelyn
Liam Ingram, her brother; early twenties
George Park, a young police constable
Young Daniel, as a boy, aged from eight to eighteen
Daniel McKennan, a visitor; mid thirties
The Man, a stranger; mid seventies

The action takes place in a rural croft, a hoolie barn on the banks of Lough Erne and a police barracks near Enniskillen, Northern Ireland

Time—Spring 1935, Autumn 1938, Summers 1955-1965, and Autumn 1985

Please note that groups performing this play must display in all announcements, publicity material and programmes the author's name, Ade Morris, and indicate that the work is based on a short story by Bryan Gallagher.

PRODUCTION NOTES

CASTING

The four characters, at different periods in their lives, may be played by two men and one woman as in the original production where one actor played young and older Daniel, and Liam, another played George and The Man and one played Maddy and Madelyn. Or, if preferred, seven actors may be used to play old and young Madelyn, George, The Man, old and young Daniel, and Liam.

SET

The play is set in a small croft on a soaking hillside near the Northern Irish border with the South in Fermanagh. The croft is small, abstracted and bare, and should have a down-at-heel appearance tempered by faded gentility. On the back wall is an old harmonium, covered by a dust cloth, beneath which is a lace runner. A piano stool stands in front. Above the harmonium is a shelf with music books, and a farm ledger of accounts. Above the shelf is a plain crucifix. In the back wall L of the harmonium is a door leading to a bedroom and pantry on the same floor (there may be steps leading to a loft bedroom also if required). R of the harmonium on the back wall is a Belfast sink with a single tap above and a water jug in the sink. R of this, on the R wall, is a set of shelves with pots, pans, plates, cups, etc., as well as Madelyn's writing box. Above, or through these shelves, streams light as from a window looking out on a small farmyard. DR of these shelves is the main entrance into the croft, with a small inner porch and a step into the yard on which characters can stand or sit. Neither of the two doorways in the original production actually had doors fitted, though this is optional. The yard beyond may be implied by lighting on or around the croft step, giving the the croft an isolated and timeless presence: an island in the dark. DR of the yard door is an old wooden dining chair with a tatty, but once fine, seat cover. In front of this chair, R in the fourth wall is an implied window with light again streaming through, this time from the lane. Another matching chair stands L, just below the bedroom door. On the wall UL are hooks for clothes and an old mirror at head height. DL is a smoking stove with chimney stretching up through an implied roof. By this stove is a pile of peat or logs, a poker, and a dustpan and brush. C stands a small traditional cottage table on which is a key.

TIME SEQUENCE
Scenes involving Daniel and the Man are set in Autumn 1985. Those
between Madelyn, George and Liam are mainly set in Spring 1935, with
the exception of the final scene between Liam and Madelyn which is
Autumn 1938. Those scenes between the young Daniel and the older
Maddy are set between the summers of 1955-1965.
 The play was originally staged with no scene breaks. The passing of
time was implied by lights, music and subtle costume changes. The idea
was to suggest how the past can live in the present, the force of memory
dictate our present lives.

MUSIC
Music, unless otherwise indicated, is used to build bridges between, and
to underscore, particular scenes or moments. The following is a list of
recorded and live music sources as used in the original and subsequent
Watermill productions of *I Dreamt I Dwelt in Marble Halls* and is
intended as a guide to mood and atmosphere. Specific songs may or may
not be adhered to, the final choice being the prerogative of the director.
Alternatively, recorded tracks used could be played live, or musicians
engaged to re-record music where appropriate.

Act I

I Dreamt that I Dwelt in Marble Halls
Taken from the intro to "I Dreamt that I Dwelt in Marble Halls" from the
opera *The Bohemian Girl* by M.W. Balfe. Played by James Galway on
the recording *Celtic Minstrel* (RCA Victor LC 0316).

She Moved Through the Fair
Taken from the intro to "She Moved Through the Fair". Played by James
Galway on the recording *Celtic Minstrel* (RCA Victor LC 0316).

I Dreamt that I Dwelt in Marble Halls
Live harmonium rendition of the tune taken from the score of *The
Bohemian Girl* by M.W. Balfe. Also sung with lyrics from the original
aria.

Garden Where the Praties Grow
Live guitar rendition of the traditional tune to "Garden Where the Praties
Grow".

Kitty's Rambles
Taken from the recording *The Irish Music Anthology: The Gold
Collection. 40 Classic Songs, Jigs and Reels*. Frank Lees Tara Cleilidh
Band (Proper/Retro R2CD 40 107/1)

Finnea Lassies
Taken from the recording *The Irish Music Anthology: The Gold
Collection. 40 Classic Songs, Jigs and Reels*. Hugh Gillespie (Proper/
Retro R2CD 40 107/1).

When the Saints Go Marching In
American Gospel/Jazz.

King Billy's March
Craigavon Protestant Boys. Taken from the recording *Auld Orange Flute
Bands* (Black Mountain Music Production BMM 0399).

Act II

Garden Where the Praties Grow
Traditional. John MacCormack's vocal recording taken from *John
McCormack — 18 Favourites*.

Carrickfergus
Traditional. Live harmonium rendition.

Irish Mist
By Boolavogue. Taken from the recording *Celtic Spirit* (Music Club
MCCD 234).

ACT I

A room in a rural croft near Enniskillen, Northen Ireland. Autumn 1985

The room is tidy but shabby: a recent coat of whitewash has tried to cover damp and dirt. There is a kitchen table C, *on which is the key to a clock. There are two wooden dining chairs with once expensive, now faded seat covers, by the side walls* L *and* R, *and a milking stool — all as if waiting to be occupied by guests. There is a door into the bedroom and pantry at the back wall* L, *and a door* R *with a porch and a step which leads to the yard. Upstage from this is a shelf area. In the back wall* R *is a Belfast sink with a single tap.* DL *is a cold hearth and pot stove and a window in the fourth wall* DR *overlooking the lane. Also on the fourth wall, approximately* C *hangs an invisible clock, the ticking of which can be heard throughout. There is a mirror* UL *and some clothes hooks with a man's cap on one hook. Against the back wall next to the sink, and underneath a dust cover, there is an old portable pedal harmonium, with a lace runner, and a piano stool. Above it is a shelf with a book of music and a ledger of farm accounts. There are various pots, pans and crockery, the paraphernalia of life in a croft, but the room is dead*

Music: "I Dreamt that I Dwelt in Marble Halls"

Daniel McKennan enters the farmyard. A man in his mid to late thirties, trim and fashionable, but clearly dressed for a funeral. His coat is particularly fine, tailored. He carries a bunch of three white roses and a guitar in a battered old guitar case. He pauses, then approaches the door. He peers tentatively in. The music fades

Daniel Is there anyone there?

No reply. Silence, he enters the room

Is there a soul in the house?

No reply. The clock in the fourth wall strikes twelve noon. He moves slowly into the room. He leans the guitar against the table, puts the roses on the table and looks around. He checks to make sure that no-one is around again, then he goes to the harmonium, uncovers it partially, and opens it. He looks around again

Well it can't hurt now ...

He tentatively makes to play a note, his back to the audience. He is pleased with the sound and experiments more, gradually he picks out the tune of "The Town I Loved So Well" and plays it tentatively at first, but with growing confidence

As he plays, The Man appears at the bedroom door. An old man, midseventies, tall, dressed darkly. A figure rooted in the past, he watches, unsmiling. He has an official bearing

The Man (*eventually interrupting*) Will you wake her inside?

Daniel abruptly stops playing, shocked

Daniel Oh Jesus I'm sorry, I thought I was the first.
The Man You are, apart from herself, and the all-seein' Lord. (*He sees the guitar*) What the feck is that?
Daniel It's a guitar ... I thought I might pl ... She's ... Miss Ingram's ...?
The Man (*indicating the bedroom*) Where else?

Silence. The Man comes closer

You play well. For a London man. You must be Daniel McKennan?
Daniel That I am, I am, yes ... (*He holds out his hand*) I always wondered how it sounded ...

The Man takes his hand

The Man I called at Morgan's, they said you'd be coming — over the water ...
Daniel What time will it be? The burial. I don't know.
The Man Half after six, she's to be carried to the priest. (*He sees the flowers*) Are they for her?
Daniel They are, they are yes ... (*An awkward moment*) ... I'm sorry, I didn't catch your name ...?
The Man They're a fine spray.
Daniel They are, for Mad ... for Miss Ingram.
The Man Could you find no red roses, man?
Daniel I remember she likes roses. I brought white, for the time ——
The Man (*speaking over Daniel*) I've seen no vase, I'll put them with her.

The Man goes back in the bedroom

Daniel (*under his breath*) Jesus ...

The Man appears in the doorway

The Man Will you take a look?
Daniel I will ... in a minute.
The Man It's a steady gaze she has. (*He comes back into the room*) How long since you saw the old lady?
Daniel Twenty years.
The Man So. You're Sally McKennan's boy, I remember your mother from Jackson's bar ...
Daniel Oh aye ...
The Man And you all London-Irish now and a big man in music over the water?
Daniel I wouldn't say that. I make my way, it's just different. How did you know her?
The Man Your mother? Or Madelyn Ingram?
Daniel Both, I suppose.
The Man Neighbours. Neighbours. I've not been back in Fermanagh long. Been away.

Silence

Daniel She reached a good age. We can say that.
The Man Can we?

Silence

Daniel She seemed old, Miss Ingram, even when I first met her.
The Man Miss Ingram?
Daniel It was Miss Ingram ...?
The Man Madelyn. That was the name I knew her by ...

Daniel is by the table. Pause, music plays very softly: "She Moved Through The Fair"

Daniel I remember ... there were chickens on this table, roosting there ...
The Man What were you doing here?
Daniel I'd come for her buttermilk, with fourpence for a can of buttermilk.

Pause

The Man It seems like she struggled.

Daniel The house was falling in then, she had no money at all.

The Man I'm sorry to hear her trouble.

Silence, except the music becomes more present. Daniel smiles to himself, a particular memory

Daniel But she was strong.

The Man She was?

Daniel She was ... I mean in herself ...

The Man Tell me ... tell me what she was like when you knew her, we've a time to pass.

Pause. Daniel meets his gaze

Come, we've a duty, 'tis a wake ...

Daniel All right. (*He takes off his coat, then, as if to the house*) Is there a soul in the house?

The music continues

The scene changes, becoming warmer, lighter, a different season and another time. Summer 1955. The room is still poor and bare, but suddenly homely

The voice of "Mad" Maddy, the older Madelyn, is heard

Maddy (*off, from the bedroom*) Is that Danny McKennan creeping on my stone?

The Young Daniel is there. He has a goose egg, wrapped in straw in a can

If older Daniel is playing his younger self then a brighter, less care-worn voice, but no attempt to actually be the boy, this is a memory

Young Daniel It is, Miss, I've come for the buttermilk, Miss.

Maddy emerges from the bedroom carrying three red roses in a vase. She puts them on the table, then she goes to the range to rattle the coals under a steaming kettle

The Man remains in the scene but is gradually placed in the distant future as the room comes alive

Daniel (*to The Man*) My mother sent me for buttermilk — once a week. I'd never seen the like of her, hair sticking out from under her hat, a man's old hat I tell you, and like a scarecrow she was ...

Maddy Will you stand there talkin' to the wall, boy, or come over for a warm? If I'd known you'd be early I'd be dressed, and be in my finery to receive you like a lady, but as it is you catch me in my poor housecoat.

Daniel .... and she had on a bag of an apron that buried what little there was of her ...

The music fades

Maddy And with nothing but a wild rose or two to brighten the place. So, give me your can.

Young Daniel Mother says to give you this, it's a goose egg, fresh laid.

Maddy Goose? (*She takes the egg*) There's a thing. I've not seen a goose's egg these eight years, not since — Marco, that met that vicious hound of Jackson's and fought him to the death.

Young Daniel Marco?

Maddy That's Marco, my old goose. Shall I tell you a story about her, boy?

Young Daniel Her? I thought you said he was called Marco; that's a man's name.

Maddy Her, that's right, and we never knew it till Marco sat for a whole week and laid an enormous egg. 'Twas like a Vatican miracle. And she was the bravest goose you ever saw, proud like a queen, or a king since she was confused on that matter, and strong like a gander, and when that hound came yelping in the yard she took him for a scoundrel and attacked him with not a thought to her fine feathers and he a big brown hunting beast that killed a hundred hare well before he set a sight upon her ... and the goose Marco just wanting to drive him away and away.

A silence, she sighs at the memory

Young Daniel You must have been terrible sad to find him, her, dead.

Maddy Marco? No! 'Twas the dog I found dead! It's neck broken like a kindlin' stick! She had a mighty wing on her, that bird — for an egg-layin' will-jill goose.

Young Daniel Will-jill?

Maddy Half William and half Jillian, a terrible confused kind of a goose.

Young Daniel What happened with her?

Maddy Jackson wanted her shot, said he'd come round with his gun and do it himself, said she was a danger to all the creatures of the earth, but I shooed him off as well ... 'Twas then about the time my brother died, and Jackson and my brother, they'd crossed each other before. But that goose was a nastier hound than his for any beggin' tinkers that peeped in the gate. (*Shouting*) Honk honk!

Music plays very softly: "She Moved Through The Fair"

Young Daniel How did she die?

Maddy Oh, it was the old age killed Marco, and that was the last goose egg I tasted the day she died ... Mind I ate Marco — God bless her, ate her entirely ... and tough as old boots she was ... I'll put this safe away.

The clock strikes one

Will you wind the clock, Daniel? (*She indicates the key on the table*)

Maddy takes the egg to the pantry

Music fades

Daniel becomes/is replaced by his older self and puts the key on the shelf above the harmonium. The Man returns. The room grows cold again. Autumn 1985. They wait in silence awhile

Daniel She told me that several times, it was a favourite.

The Man Is it true, do you think?

Daniel Why should she lie?

The Man Aye, or anyone ... (*He looks through the door, down the hill*) I can't think we'll be the only mourners.

Daniel No.

The Man And you with no lick of a drink about ye? ... To keep the spirits flowing ... Did you bring a drop?

Daniel Drink?... No I didn't think ...

The Man London Irish ...

Daniel says nothing

Warm lager in Irish theme pubs, you're severed from decent drinkin' like a hand from an Irish arm.

Daniel That's not really true ...

The Man No? (*He pulls an opened bottle of Irish whiskey from his coat pocket and puts it on the table*) There's a bottle if you'd like, I thought to bring it.
Daniel You did?

Silence

Well a drink might be nice.
The Man Nice? It's a wake, boy — what else is there to do?
Daniel I'd love a drink. God, you make a man nervous, you know.

The Man takes a swig from the bottle, wipes it, offers it to Daniel

I'll find a glass.

Silence. Daniel returns with glasses

She had no more friends? That might come ...?
The Man She was the loneliest creature on the banks of Lough Erne.
Daniel But you saw her yourself?
The Man Like I said, I'm not long here, from Londonderry.
Daniel Derry?... Yes I always meant to come back here but, well, I was away, beyond, there was never the chance.
The Man Chance is a fine thing, it makes a mock of us. Do you mind this one was reared in elegance, carpets on the floor, nothing but the best. They lived in a grand farmhouse and had plenty for the time ...
Daniel I heard that too.
The Man You did? It's a small town with a big mouth full of flappin' tongues.

Music: "I Dreamt that I Dwelt in Marble Halls"

Maddy comes in again, as if alone in the ruined parlour. She stares at the roses

Daniel I heard she was the belle of the county, in her day, quite some beauty ...
The Man (*pouring the whiskey*) Dressed always in the latest fashion, and come Sunday people would stare at her just for the joy of staring as she rode her way to mass in a pony and trap ... with her little harmonium behind her. (*He pours Daniel's drink*) There you go ...
Daniel (*taken aback by the fullness of the picture*) Did she have no family then? I never knew.

The Man None living. Parents gone a long time off. There was a
  brother.

The Man knocks back his whiskey, grimaces. Daniel sips

Daniel You must have known him?
The Man No, no, I knew his face. They said he was a good neighbour.
  a hunting man he was, kept a pair of hounds, farmed. (*Indicating the
  harmonium*) She'd give lessons on that thing. (*He examines the bottle*)
  This is hard stuff ... I'll fetch some water ...

*The Man puts the whisky bottle on the shelf by the sink and fetches a
jug of water. Maddy turns to the harmonium. The warm room gradually
returns*

  Spring water, mind! You'd pay good money for that in London ...
Daniel You would!

The Man pours water in Daniel's whiskey

The Man London Irish, now that's a different manner of man
  altogether ...
Daniel Och I don't know, the old country ... it's all very w ——
The Man The old country, where would that be then? Somewhere dead
  and gone is it? Where is the dusty place?
Daniel Well ...

Pause

The Man So. We've a duty here to fulfil, 'tis a wake after all ... and a
  poor business ... Here's to her, what was it, "the belle of the county".
Daniel To her — to Miss Ingram, that I knew.
The Man May the angels take her back ...

They drink

  Will you talk more of her? Tell me what she was like, when you met
  her first ... how she was — since we're to put her to rest.

Daniel takes a drink, decides to humour the man

Daniel All right. Well, I could hear her singing ...
The Man Singing? By the love of God.

Daniel I stood there outside, by the dung hill, I was eight, nine maybe, it's there still but grassed over — and I listened, she was singing an old song , "I Dreamt that I" ——
The Man — "Dwelt in Marble Halls" ...
Daniel I've never forgotten.
The Man *The Bohemian Girl.*
Daniel The opera?
The Man The film! Laurel and Hardy! It's as funny a picture as you'll see.
Daniel I've not seen it ... It was the song about the dreaming, and loving still the same.
The Man I know it, bless her voice, Rosy Lawrence sang it in the film. (*He uncovers the harmonium completely*) A little princess is kidnapped by gypsies and loses her kingdom — loses everything — but she gets to live with Laurel and Hardy so it's not all bad.

He begins to play, picking out the notes of "I Dreamt that I Dwelt in Marble Halls", the recorded music fades to be replaced by the harmonium

Daniel That's it ... It was a sweet noise to come from such a broken-down place, and it rooted me stock still, you didn't expect to hear such a thing there, you know, like a cough in a graveyard ...

Daniel turns away, and as he does Maddy haltingly sings the first line, as if prompted by the harmonium

The young Daniel stands in the doorway and Maddy sings, his memory of her alive. Maddy becomes more and more involved as she sings — stiffly acting out the song

Maddy   I dreamt I dwelt in marble halls
with vassels and serfs at my side
and of all who assembled within those walls
that I was the hope and the pride.
I had riches all too great to count
and high ancestral name.
But I also dreamt which pleased me most
that you loved me still the same,
that you loved me
you loved me still the same
that you loved me
you loved me still the same.

> I dreamt that suitors sought my hand,
> that knights upon bended knee
> and with vows no maiden's heart could withstand,
> they pledged their faith to me.
> And I dreamt that one of that noble host
> came forth my hand to claim.
> But I also dreamt which charmed me most
> that you loved me still the same,
> that you loved me
> you loved me still the same
> that you loved me
> you loved me still the same.

The Man gently stops playing and closes the harmonium, Maddy is quite bewitched by herself. She is down on her knees in the hearth

Young Daniel Miss Ingram?

Maddy makes a futile attempt to hide behind the table

  Miss Ingram?

She braves it, stands

Maddy Can't you knock on the door like a normal body?
Young Daniel I'm sorry, I was listening ——
Maddy Listening, was it? Then a fine old wailing you heard!
Young Daniel It was lovely.
Maddy And you with a liar's silver tongue in your head. You know about music, do you? A fine judge? Do they teach you that in school, or just cursin' and fightin'?
Young Daniel I know a bit. I like music ... You must know a bit ... I heard you gave lessons.
Maddy I know enough to make a noise. Now then, you'll be here for the buttermilk. Do you have fourpence?
Young Daniel I do.
Maddy Then put it on the table. And don't be letting on you know a thing about what you heard here.
Young Daniel If you like, why should I not tell, why not?

She goes close to him, very intense, almost a little mad

Maddy There's a wind of gossip in this place, you hear it in the trees sometimes. Birds with beaks and beady eyes.

Young Daniel I won't tell ——

Maddy And you be going away, my boy, as soon as your legs are long and strong ... Be gone from this place and beyond — and never come back while I'm still the green side of the turf. Do you promise me that — do you?

Young Daniel I do, I promise.

Maddy Good. Good boy. Give me your can for the milk. (*She takes the can, goes for the buttermilk, turns back*) So. And a music scholar are you? Which might you prefer then, John McCormack, or Gigli?

Music plays very softly: "She Moved Through The Fair"

Maddy returns to the pantry

Daniel (*as his older self to The Man*) And that was the start of it, me the wee boy and Mad Madelyn Ingram.

The Man They called her mad? Poor Madelyn ...

Daniel And she never stopped telling me to go away, to take the train, find a fortune over the water, until I did, and of course I'd never really meant to keep that promise but ... But you get so busy over there, there's a different pace.

The Man So I hear, sure you must live quick lives in England, you'd live ten of them for one good life in Ireland, like a hound, and likely be ten times less happy for it too ...

Daniel It suits me.

The Man You saw her every week?

During the following, Maddy sheds her older self, becomes young and beautiful, she removes her hat, her old bag apron, reveals a pretty dress and shakes down long rich hair, it should be a magical but simple transformation

Daniel Pretty much, over the years I'd hear more about how she had been, how she was such a beauty ——

The Man She was ...

Daniel — just like you said, that there was none good enough to woo her, how she'd play the men like roosters all off against each other.

The Man laughs

The Man Roosters was it?

Daniel And lead them all to dance and fight ... how she had a wastrel brother ...

The Man Did she by God! I'm away for a piss, if you'll excuse me
— and get some good clean air in my lungs.

*The Man strolls out into the yard, closing the door behind him. Out
of sight, he is replaced by/becomes transformed into the young police
constable, George*

The music increases in volume

*It is Spring 1935. A bicycle bell rings. The music fades. Daniel becomes/
is replaced by Liam. Georges's voice is heard behind the croft*

George (*off*) I know you're in there, Liam Ingram!

*Sudden frantic actvity as Madelyn tries to prepare for a visitor and Liam
makes to hide himself*

Liam gets himself a glass of water, gulps down two

Madelyn Oh Liam, you're back, where the devil have you been?
Liam Does it matter?
George (*off*) Will you come to the door? I can see the chimney
smokin'!

Another ring

   George appears on his bicycle

Liam Madelyn there's a ringin' outside will split my head!
Madelyn Do you think I'm deaf as well as half daft! Well you're my
own brother so you'll have the same affliction by and by.

Another ring. George is standing his bicycle, straightening his clothing

Liam My head, Maddy! Spare it!
Madelyn Oh, listen to the poor darlin'! A wild roving man with no
thought to the farm or anything but the taste of neat spirit — and the
spending and spilling of his own ...

Another ring

Liam Just help me out, Maddy!
Madelyn Quiet yourself, Liam!

She pushes Liam into the bedroom

I'm coming!

She comes to the half-door, opens it, and sees George

Constable Park! Well you're as welcome as flowers in May. Will you come in?
George I will, for a time, I've a way to go.

George comes in. He is a handsome young policeman, but awkward, caught between the uniform and the man, he stands and stares. Madelyn is over gallant and determined to make light of his visit. She verges on flirtatious, but this is just the way she is, not a tease or affectation

Pause

Madelyn Well now. Shall I guess what brings you three miles on that torturing old bike to our door ...?

George is still silent, or rather at a loss

George Well ...
Madelyn (*leaping in*) Sure you've come to arrest me for robbing the Bank of Ireland with a starting pistol last week! A desperate crime by a desperate brave-hearted woman...?

George almost speaks but is interrupted

Or is it the pig smuggling you've come after me for? There's whole pens of southern pigs held hostage in the bedroom if you'll take a look, all snortin' for mercy from the clutches of desperados like myself ...

A short pause. She waits for him to gather his speech

George It's about your brother Liam I'm here.
Madelyn Sure he's killed a man! I knew it by the bloody weapon in his hand and the mad glint of his eye as he lay in his bloodstained bed this whole morning snoring and snortin' — like the pigs in the bedroom there.

She leans into the bedroom where Liam is hiding and she snorts like a pig

George Will you listen to me speak, Miss Ingram?

Madelyn Why certainly.

George There's been a complaint from Jackson at the bar ... He says that Liam — well that he, was drunk last night and ——

Madelyn Liam drunk! Surely there must be a mistake! Liam Ingram — the very ramrod of piety and teetotal highfalutin manners, drunk in a town bar. Sir, you have offended me, I swoon ...

George (*annoyed at last, dropping the formality*) For Christ's sake, Miss Ingram, you're not at The Derry Waterside now! — Will you take the tongue from your head and sit upon it before it wags itself to death!

Madelyn (*serious suddenly*) How much does he want?

George He says three pounds, there's a window broken, and a chair smashed on the head of poor John Reece.

Madelyn He's a rock hard head, it's no wonder the chair broke, but three pounds is a neat sum for an evening's work ...

George He says he'll take no less; there's a quantity of drink spilled too.

Madelyn I don't have it, George. There he lies up in his bed. You'll be taking him to the town for this, and locking him away with crooks and criminals, and him under the doctor.

George Let me speak with him, let him get some air in his lungs.

Madelyn Hush now, George, and go away the while till he can be spoken to. He's in no state for talking or walking with you after a night like the last. Did you see how he laid into Reece?

George I did. There's times when it's a mortal hazard to wear the tunic, and when there's temper mixed with drink that's one of them, best to let the two work on each other, and no harm done — except that poor chair, and Reece's head.

Madelyn You're a wise man, Constable George Park, and a good policeman too ...

George Well, thanks for that.

Madelyn A pleasure as always. But Jackson being a Unionist and Liam in the mood he is ... God their hounds fight on the hunt so the men are just the same.

George Aye, men and hounds are very alike when they're being chased.

Madelyn There, that's so.

George But there's a thing I have to say as well. I'll be back in London-derry myself too soon, they'll be makin' me a sergeant ——

Madelyn That's grand!

George And the next constable mayn't be so — gentle ... Will you speak with Liam then?

Madelyn Of course I will, but I don't know what he'll do.
George Then I'll go, and er — see you soon I hope.

He makes to leave but she stops him

Madelyn What's that you say about leaving soon, to Derry, I mean, and you to be a sergeant?
George That's right, 'tis a promotion I've been hoping for but ... Well they want me back in the city, and they say it takes a Catholic to spread the law in South Fermanagh.
Madelyn Is the law a Catholic then? Sure I thought the law was an atheist heathen devil through and through ...
George That's your brother talkin'. I'll go. Tell him I'm at the station.
Madelyn Yes go ... and be well missed.
George Aye?
Madelyn Aye. And leave us desperate criminals to contemplate our terrible crime.
George You're one for the words, Miss Ingram, always were. (*He is almost gone, but suddenly finds courage*) I'll be calling at the hoolie a week Friday, after the hunt ... Were you thinking of going?
Madelyn Well, we'll see, I fancy a dance, and the hoolie's a good bit of crack — and I thought I might sing ... But by Friday we might have fled to the Americas, along with every other Catholic the wrong side of your Derry law.

She takes his hat, and puts it on. He makes an attempt to get it back but fails

George Can I please have my hat back, Miss Ingram?
Madelyn (*still teasing him*) Take it, why don't you?

George takes the hat and leaves, smiling. Liam emerges from behind the bedroom door

Madelyn takes the roses from the table and holds them to her nose. Liam looks terrible, a different mood is struck, much more mundane and down to earth. As they speak Liam takes out his guitar and starts to play "Gardens Where the Praties Grow" roughly. He leaves the guitar case on the table

Liam What did he want? A sniff of your rose bush?
Madelyn (*annoyed*) You, Liam, in irons, if you don't pay for the damage last night.

Liam Why should I pay? There was more than me in the quarrel.
Madelyn But it was you that turned to your fists.
Liam That's a fine-sounding thing to say, Maddy, but if every blow had a price there'd be poor men all over the six counties, and that's surely not so.
Madelyn There you go ahead, will you leave it be and keep your chin from other men's fists? Besides you shouldn't drink, 'tis bad for your diabetes ...

Madelyn closes and replaces the guitar case

Liam Don't school me, Maddy! You're trying so hard to be English there's butter frozen on your tongue; 'tis a hard thing to be the brother of a stuck-up girl like yourself.
Madelyn It's a hard thing, is it? The hardest thing in this house is the baked brown nut of your brain. (*She takes the cap from his head and belts him with it*) You owe John Jackson three pounds. I haven't even three thrupenny bits and you don't lift a finger. What are we to do, Liam?
Liam I'll sell two pigs at the next fair!
Madelyn And then there's two less ... Better to keep two pigs than those two hounds?
Liam You'd have a poor hunt with pigs instead of hounds!
Madelyn Liam ...
Liam God, Maddy, they breed. Have you not seen them at it, likely they even enjoy it! (*He snorts like a pig*)

Madelyn leaves, exasperated

The clock strikes twice. The cold kitchen returns

Liam becomes/is replaced by Daniel, the guitar playing evolves into Daniel practising the melody of "I Dreamt that I Dwelt in Marble Halls"

The Man returns

Daniel notices The Man and stops playing

Daniel Did you wind the clock?
The Man I did, yes I did.

Pause

Daniel I used to wind it for her, it's a good fast tick.
The Man Will you take another drink, Elvis?
Daniel I will, thanks.

A lively jig begins, the start of the hunt-house hoolie

  *In another time Madelyn can be seen preparing for the dance in front
  of her mirror, practising steps*

  She was aiming too high they said ...
The Man Was she, by God?
Daniel And always on the look-out for the right manner of man ...
The Man (*refilling Daniel's glass*) Is that so? The right manner of
  man?
Daniel It's what I heard.
The Man There's a fierce gossip in this town, and this all fifty year
  ago ...
Daniel And her wanting away to the arms of escape, but never finding
  a ticket would take her there.
The Man Not like yourself?
Daniel But they said she'd been led to a place above her station by her
  Ma and Da — elocution lessons and all.
The Man She spoke well, I remember.
Daniel And the man on foot she didn't want, and the man on horseback
  passed her by.
The Man What?
Daniel A saying I heard ...
The Man It's a terrible thing, to look and see all there is to have, but
  never to have it.

*Much laughter and excitement and applause for the band as the hoolie
room becomes real*

Daniel becomes/is replaced by Liam and takes the stage

Madelyn hands Liam the guitar

The Man becomes/is replaced by George

Liam That's it, right, now quieten down! Quieten down! Now can
  I introduce Madelyn Ingram! With something you might half
  recognize!

Madelyn stands as though surrounded by admirers, a smattering of applause and good natured heckling. Liam accompanies her as she recites her comic poem, in a very mock-English voice. The chorus is sung by Madelyn, in a music-hall style, to the traditional tune of "Garden Where the Praties Grow"

Madelyn (*reciting*) I've got so many lovers
                         I don't know which to choose,
                         for love is such a sweet old game,
                         I am most loath to lose —
                         For what if my eventual choice
                         should be missing his hair and his teeth?

Liam Like you, Eddie.

Laughter

Madelyn (*reciting*) And instead of a large
                         and refined country seat,
                         I find that my home
                         is on poverty street ...
                         ... and my husband's a rogue
                         with ten children to keep
                         ... from his other six wives
                         who all died in their sleep ...

Liam begins to play. George happily claps along with everyone else

   (*Singing*)   Oh I've got so many lovers
                         I don't know which to choose
                         for love is such a sweet old game
                         I am most loath to lose
                         I do not care to love you quick
                         I'd rather love you slow ...
All   So meet me in the garden
                         where the praties grow!

Madelyn interrupts the clapping

Madelyn Or ...
   (*Reciting*)   What if my eventual choice
                         should be missing a brain in his head ——

Liam Like a peeler!

Laughter. George stands, and looks around in a good-natured way to see who's laughing

Madelyn (*reciting*) — and thinks with his feet
to leave me and the wain
for some other poor girl instead,
that's prettier, wittier, and flutters her eyes
to tempt him along to her bed ...

(*Singing*) Ach I've got so many lovers
I don't know which to choose
for love is such a sweet old game
I am most loath to lose
I do not care to love you quick
I'd rather love you slow.
All So meet me in the garden
where the praties grow!

Madelyn interrupts the clapping

Madelyn Or ...
(*Reciting*) Perhaps I'll leave old love alone
and be content, like a hound with a bone
to bury my heart
in a garden, fair
and no-one will know
it lies beating there,

George Poor Miss Ingram ...

Madelyn (*reciting*) except all the praties and flowers that grow
on all the love lost ...
ach 'twill be quite a show.

Liam plays again

All (*singing*) Oh I've got so many lovers
I don't know which to choose
for love is such a sweet old game
I am most loath to lose
I do not care to love you quick

> I'd rather love you slow...
> So meet me in the garden
> where the praties grow!

As everyone sings the following, Madelyn stands on the table and does a little dance

> Oh I've got so many lovers
> I don't know which to choose
> for love is such a sweet old game
> I am most loath to lose
> I do not care to love you quick
> I'd rather love you slow...
> So meet me in the garden
> where the praties grow!

A round of applause and calls of "Again!" as Madelyn takes a theatrical bow and descends. The band tunes up amidst calls for "More!". Liam is quick to leap to Madelyn's side

Liam No, she'll speak no more tonight and thank you all, there's dancin' now for dancers with the Starlight Dance Band — thanks Bryan, John — and drinkin' for all you with only two left feet!

Madelyn Come dance with me, Liam, or there'll be a desperate fight for my hand.

Liam Come on then.

The music grows louder as the band begin to play "Kitty's Rambles" followed by "Finnea Lassies". Madelyn and Liam dance with much whooping and laughter and George watches them. She breaks away as Liam also reels to the bar and she comes to George

They move outside on to the forestage and the music fades to interior. Liam stands in the doorway, watching the dance within but keeping an eye on Madelyn

Night by the loughside

Madelyn You're not dancing tonight then, Constable?

George I'm watching — Miss Ingram, and there's much in it for thought. I enjoyed your recital there ...

Madelyn Thank you. And what are your thoughts then, Constable? Since we're so formal perhaps you should put them to writing?

George No, no, I'm no writer, but while we're out here there's a thought that nags my mind that's hard to speak ...

Madelyn Try then, see what you can muster, what's the thought most like? Is it a dog or a cat, or a bird or a fish in the lough or what?

George Well ... It's a — slippery thing of a thought with neither an arm nor a leg to catch a hold of.

Madelyn Sounds a mightily fishy thought — not one to sniff or hold ...

George No, no, it's not fishy, not fishy at all!

Madelyn Is it a thought about me, or your man in there, Liam — since that's where your eyes are pointing?

George You? Perhaps it is yes. Perhaps I'm wondering who you'll be marrying, and myself too, since we live in a place where the choice is neither large nor small ...?

Madelyn Well that is a thought. I've little enough idea on that ...

George There's not a man on the lough wouldn't marry you, Madelyn — you know that — including half the ones that are married already. I'd marry you myself — to put you out of your misery you understand, if I didn't have to go to Londonderry again ...

Madelyn Why thank you, 'tis good you take pity on a poor country girl ... But sure you think I'll be swept away by any of those new potatoes at the bar. I'm as like to marry you as any of them, and I know you too well for that ...

George That's true, and friends should never marry, no it sends the taste right off, like lemon in milk ... No 'twould never do ... So tell me what's the stamp of the man you'll take?

Madelyn Oh he must be charming, witty, handsome ... fierce rich, a man of property and position, a man whose arm is a pretty place for a girl to hang and be watched by all who pass.

George Is there such a man in Ireland?

Madelyn There are many, I'm sure of it, though not so many you'd see one dancing here tonight ...

George I'm thinking you'll be marrying a fine Englishman, and leaving this place for beyond?

Madelyn Perhaps. There's not much here for a bold girl to love, unless she's a passion for bacon and green grass, or water instead of wine.

George And not much love in this match, if all it takes is a square jaw and a purse full of English pounds to turn a pretty head.

Madelyn Oh there's a fine attraction in a fat purse! You know, it can't be so very hard to love a rich man, even if his face is like a pig's behind ...

George laughs

Oh but you'll have no problem with the ladies, Constable — being but a man ... and no sign of a pig about you ...

George Well I would rather be a lonely man than a pig's arse, no matter how rich ... But think of this ... What if you have no choice at all of who you love ...? What if you get struck with love one star-filled night for a pimple-faced office boy that's blown into town on the Omagh bus that morning?

Madelyn That's destiny you're talkin' of, but my destiny's all my own, George ... I don't believe in life being all mapped out before you ever start it, no, what you do is what you get ... and who I love will be my own choice.

George Except your brother, there's a love you can't avoid.

Madelyn It's a different thing, a blood relation. I love a dog as well because it's mine. But Liam can look after himself.

George 'Twill take a great effort ...

The music grows louder again

Madelyn And now I must be back to the dance, or they'll all say I will be marrying you, Constable. I leave you to your slippery fish ...

George I'll never land it, Madelyn, there's nothing so certain in my head.

Madelyn is away. The dance intensifies, then fades

George, Madelyn and Liam exit

The croft room returns. Later that night

Madelyn enters, singing to herself and dancing slowly around. It is late. The night passes as she speaks

Madelyn "I've got so many lovers I don't know which to choose." (*She stops by the mirror*) I've got so many ... Look at yourself. Just look at yourself, you silly girl. Mother in your face. Written all over ... Come back, Mammy, let's see you. (*She arranges her hair like her mother's*) There. There you are. Well, you were the same, Mammy, or there wouldn't be such a thing as me at all ... Married the best man you could find and so if he was a farmer ... "The first precious" — no, "the most precious thing a woman has is the first thing to lose, and that should be your looks not your fortune" ... True enough. But Daddy said it was silly. Well, he would. (*She takes her daddy's hat, rams it on her head like Maddy. Talking to the chair*) You listen to me, Miss Madelyn Ingram. Men, men are like guns, very liable to go off any time and hurt you bad. You're a pretty girl, Madelyn, but don't let it go to your head ...

She moves to the window. It grows lighter

Ach this place, Mullyneeny, Toneywall, Knockninny, and the whole mountain soaking with water. I'd lick the road to get away, I would, with my bare tongue, I would ... Like — George Park, off to Derry to be a sergeant ...

The following morning

George arrives on his bicycle, he rings his bell

Whoever's there you're welcome here, come in will you.

George enters and takes off his cap

Constable Park ... Your ears must be raw red.

George It's a cold day, yes ...

Madelyn You're a regular here, and no harm in it. Well now, anything new or strange?

George I've come to see Liam again, if he's in.

Madelyn He's down the field with the bull, trying to entice him to old Hanly's cow.

George Sure that cow must be a hundred years old if it's a day?

Madelyn Yes. And had her fill of bulls. 'Twill take more than Liam's whistling to make the bull rise to it. There's a power of words to be said for natural attraction, don't you think, Constable?

George Oh there is, though it's hard for a bull when all the cows look the same ... and particularly when it comes to a cow like old Hanly's, there's bare difference between one end and the other. So, I'm with the bull on that one.

Madelyn Constable!

George Call me George, won't you? You do betimes, but you're forever seeing the uniform ...

Madelyn Yes well, you're forever round here wearing it! Do you want me to see the man? Then take it off — then see how you shiver ...

George Aye well, what if I did?

Pause

Madelyn Aye well, what if you did?

Pause. George blushes, to his credit

George Well 'tis true, it would be cold.

*Liam comes in, not in good humour. He has a package under his arm,
a small heavy bundle which contains a corked bottle of poteen*

*Liam puts the bundle on a chair in the corner. Madelyn looks at it
disapprovingly*

Liam (*taking a ledger from the shelf and putting two bills from his pocket
into it*) Constable Park! Have you no criminal to be chasin' on your
old bike out there? They'll stand no chance with you in pursuit on the
Fermanagh thunderbolt ... Is there tea made, Maddy? I'm parched.

George Sure you're as bad as each other. I came to see you, there's a
matter to discuss.

Madelyn I'll make some, there's a kettle near boiled.

*During the following, she makes tea and brings a tray of tea things to
the table*

Liam Me, is it? Well, I'm all yours, it's a fine day when a man can't
walk into his own kitchen without the arms of the law to greet him and
not his loving sister.

Madelyn Liam! Don't take on with George, he's only passing the
time ...

George Well no, as a matter of fact, it is the law that brings me here.

Liam (*to Madelyn*) I thought so much when I saw his flinty face.

George There's the matter of a complaint from Jackson.

Liam The man's a scandalous liar.

George He's still black and blue, like Reece.

Liam Red white and blue more like.

An awkward silence

Madelyn Will you take sugar — Constable?

George Is that the reason behind this?

Liam I wish it was, but the truth is the man upset my mood, and I've a
fierce bad temper when it comes to an insult.

George Aye well. The thing is he wants you to make amends with
three pound for the damage to the bar, and not to come near the place
again.

Madelyn Will you take a seat, Constable?

George No, I'm fine.

Liam Well the second I'll gladly do, but as to the first he'll have to be
sorry too, and say it to my own face before I pay a penny.

Madelyn Liam, will you not just pay the man and have done ... You
were selling stock to do it when I asked you last.

Liam That I did, but there's better things to buy than Jackson's good will.

Madelyn You spent it, you didn't give him the money?

Liam Yes, well I've no mind to do that any more, I've thought about it and that's my answer. Is that an arrestable offence, Constable?

George No, no. Unless he brings charges and he's not done that. But I'm thinking it's not the right thing to do, and this is a small town not to go near the best bar for ten mile about ...

Liam I wouldn't step near the place, the man's got blue blood and a Protestant as well. I wouldn't spit on his grave — sure I wouldn't feckin dig it first.

Madelyn Will you listen to yourself! If our mammy could hear you talk ...

Liam If our mother could hear him talk, your man Reece, with Jackson laughing him on, and about the likes of you, then she'd spin in her grave like a jenny.

George What about her? What about your sister?

Liam I could not repeat it. But now you know the reason for it, and no more nor less.

Madelyn What did he say?

Liam Does it matter?

George No, it does not. Forget it.

Madelyn It matters to me!

Liam It matters to me!

Madelyn So tell me what it is that means I need defending by you, you great turnip.

Liam Well for sure I won't take the trouble next time. I'll lead the chorus instead!

George Oh, listen to the two of you.

They stop

I'll have a word with Jackson, try to calm him down.

Liam Aye, and tell him he's as much chance of seeing his three pound as he has of seeing my face in his stinkin' English bar again.

George Well on that point I'm sure he'll be much relieved ... (*He starts to leave*)

Liam That is till I want a drink and he's nearest, then he'll taste my fist again.

Madelyn Be quiet, Liam!

George pauses

George I did not hear that, Liam.

Liam I said I'd clock him one again if he opens his mouth!

George comes back, a hard stare and silence

George Is that a threat of violence, Liam?
Liam What if it is? 'Tis not to you.

Silence

Madelyn Oh, for pity's sake will you listen to each other, they'll ring
the playtime bell any minute and give you both warm milk.
Liam Will you keep out of this, Maddy!

Silence

George What do you want me to do, Liam? Is it me you'll be fightin'
next?
Liam I reckon. I don't see why that uniform should make you harder to
hit, and you a feckin' Protestant to boot — and well worth the belt.
George You lay a finger on me, Liam Ingram, and you lay a finger on
the law of this land and there's a consequence there to consider.
Madelyn No, George, go. He's just a stupid boy.
Liam (*with real violence in his voice*) Shut up, Maddy!

*George and Liam stare again, a real confrontation, but George is
compromised by the presence of Madelyn, and by his uniform*

George Liam. I'm going to turn round and I'm going to walk out that
door. And try to forget that this ever happened. (*To Madelyn*) Good-
day to you.

George turns and slowly leaves

*Liam does not move. He has understood that he pushed the confrontation
a little too far. Liam and Madelyn are left alone*

Madelyn You should surely not have done that, Liam.
Liam He's one of them, he's ——
Madelyn He's George! He's my friend, he's our friend.
Liam Your friend! Yes and every other man with a fancy suit of clothes
in the county!

Silence between them

Madelyn What in the devil's name did the man Reece say?

Silence again

Well?
Liam He said you're a bounty hunter. And think yourself better than all the rest. And when he heard you'd sing at the hoolie ——
Madelyn Yes ...
Liam He said: "Aye there's some hoor singin', and some hoor not."

Pause. Madelyn takes it in

Madelyn And that's why you hit him.
Liam That and the strong will to plug that northern gobshite's hole for every other word he says.

Pause

Madelyn And what do you think, yourself?
Liam You know what I think: I think myself you should be less about with airs and graces and favour; 'tis a small little town and people with noses as long as prize parsnips.

Pause

Madelyn I hate this place. It pulls me down like a bird in lime. There's such a jealous streak ... I want more than there is.
Liam Here we go then ...
Madelyn Liam, listen.
Liam I've heard the song before, Maddy.
Madelyn That doesn't make it less true! Look, Liam, why don't we sell the farm and go. There's nothing to stop us. What's here but a pack of gossips and put-you-downs who've always hated the likes of us?
Liam This is our land, Maddy, our place.
Madelyn No, Liam, it's just the place our daddy chose to live, we could've been in Galway or County Down, wherever, and Mam just came along. We've no loyalty to pay them, they're gone, Mam and Da, we can go anywhere we want, you and me.
Liam They worked hard for us.
Madelyn But it's slipping away, Liam, don't you see that? Everything we thought we had is less than we had a year ago. You're no more right for this life than I am, they brought us up all wrong for here, and Reece and Jackson, they're right. I do want more, but I don't have

any shame in that! God, Liam, you could work in an office in Derry, you can think, you don't have to be leading bored bulls to clapped-out cows!

Liam unwraps the corked bottle of illegal poteen

Liam I can't leave, Maddy.
Madelyn Why not? Just give me a reason.
Liam Because it'd feel like we're being driven out, giving in.
Madelyn Who to, Jackson and that eejit John Reece?
Liam No, them. The north!
Madelyn Liam, this isn't about that. This is the north ...We're just people living here, with other people, like anywhere.
Liam No, Maddy, we're not. Will you get me a cup?
Madelyn Get your own cup!
Liam (*getting one, pouring a cup, drinking it*) There's no such thing as people just living their lives, we're all a part of something else and it can't be got away from. There's a struggle ...
Madelyn Listen to yourself! You'll be in the IRA next! What's happening to you? Why do you have to believe all that? Where's my little brother gone?

Silence. They have reached a point of no going back

Liam I don't want you seeing the constable any more.
Madelyn What?
Liam You heard me, Maddy.
Madelyn You've no place to ask me such a thing ...
Liam I'm your brother.
Madelyn Not my keeper!
Liam It's for your good.
Madelyn My good? I doubt that! Leave me be, Liam, you'll not cross me.
Liam And you must keep inside more; I can't fight the whole town to keep your name clean.
Madelyn You think I'll live like a nun because you tell me? God! — Tell Sally Mckennen that, Liam, or any other bar-fly down at Jackson's, or is that different, Liam? Sure, she's not your sister now, is she?
Liam I'm asking.

She is furious. Outside it begins to rain and there is the sound of rain on the tin roof

Madelyn I want none of this, Liam Ingram! I'm my own spirit, do you hear? And if I choose to sing and dance and be myself and maybe land a fine husband on the way that's my life — and my soul I'm setting a fire to, and as for you and your petty fists you can beat them in the face of every man that tries to kiss me but they'll all be like rocks to you, you petty-minded jealous ——

Liam (*interrupting her*) That's a fine speech, Maddy!

Madelyn Is it a wonder that I want to get from this place and your clay-footed clinging? God you make me mad, Liam — and the Holy Church forgive me ...

Liam It's for your good, Maddy.

Madelyn Oh God!

Madelyn pushes past Liam and rushes out

Liam Maddy! Don't take on ...

The rain gets worse; it drums on the tin roof of the croft

(*Calling after her from the doorway*) So you'll be wanting a fine husband, Maddy! Well there's more to a marriage than choosing ... and you'll wish for a brother's company when the wains are all cryin' in the night and another one on the way … (*He picks up the bottle*) Like poor old Shona McGuire that's never a day older than yourself but looks near fifty with the hips and jugs on her! Can you hear me, Maddy?... Are you there?... Ah be gone with you, and a wet night too to damp your fire ... (*He strides back into the room, grabs the cup and bottle and returns to the door*) Poteen in a china cup! (*He returns to the table, collects himself and holds up the bottle and cup*) Now there's a tidy bride and groom to make the church bell ring. (*He pours a large shot into the teacup*) These that God has joined together let no man tear asunder ... (*He smiles to himself, drinks*)

The rain gets worse

Liam takes his bottle and teacup with saucer into the bedroom, leaving two on the table with the teapot, etc.

As the rain pours there is the terrible noise of George practising "When the Saints Go Marching In" badly on a cornet. The Lights change to indicate George's first-floor rooms at the barracks

Playing the cornet and in shirt-sleeves, George enters from the bedroom

George Come on, George!

Another failed attempt at the tune

Madelyn calls to him from outside beneath the window (on the forestage) but he cannot hear her

Madelyn (*off*) Constable Park! Constable Park!

Unable to hear Madelyn, George continues playing. Madelyn throws stones at the window

(*Off*) George!

A gap in the cornet playing

(*Off*) George!
George (*leaning out of the window*) Miss Ingram! You're dripping wet! Will you come on up out of it, it's wild out there. (*He puts the cornet on the table*)

Madelyn enters, dripping wet, through the croft (now barracks) door

George is embarrassed. During the following, he casts around for a jacket to put on, then realizes she needs it more than him and puts it around her shoulders

Madelyn Thank you...
George Here, come and warm yourself. I'll make myself decent. (*He fastens his shirt*) I was expecting no-one, it's late, but you're welcome. Will you have a cup of hot tea? There's a brew on.
Madelyn I can't go back there.
George What's the matter? What is it, Madelyn?
Madelyn Do you have a drop of the hard stuff?
George Lord's sakes, what's he done?
Madelyn No, no he's done nothing, he's not hurt me, he'd never do that.
George There's whiskey. I'll fetch it then you tell me what it is that troubles you.

George takes the tea tray from the table and fetches the whiskey and two shot glasses from the shelf. Madelyn looks around. She has never been here before

Madelyn I didn't know you played that thing.
George What, the cornet? I'm still learnin'. There's a marchin' band they'll want me in, you know, when I get back ... I enjoy it
Madelyn Are you an Orangeman, Constable?
George I was in a lodge — but I just like the noise of it, and the crack of it. There's little enough to do off duty for a bachelor in barracks.

He pours whiskey into the glasses. They drink. There is a silence, but not an awkward one

Madelyn There's sweet stuff. Will you play me a note?
George Oh you don't want that — it's a terrible din, and you're drippin'.
Madelyn I do! Please.
George Never! I tell you what, music teacher, I'll give you a free lesson in playing it for yourself.
Madelyn I thought you were a learner too?
George I am that, but teachin's as difficult as learnin', always was, so I may as well do one as the other.

He hands her the instrument

  That's it now take it there, and there, hold it firm.
Madelyn Like this?
George Well, you'll be wanting it the other way round.
Madelyn I know!

She follows his direction. He sits close by her to show her the method, but there is an innocence about it

  And I blow in here?
George That's it, but press down this one and this, that'll make a note. There, now purse your lips like you're going to kiss a baby and blow.

Madelyn does as she is told. She goes very red in the face but nothing happens except a strangled farting which she repeats several times

Madelyn This is harder than it looks.
George Take a rest and a sip, your face is awful red!
Madelyn It's the blood in me.
George Here. (*He raises his glass*) Er — to the future.

They clink their glasses. Another drink and short silence

Madelyn He doesn't understand me even half at all, what I want from
my life.

George I thought that'd be it. He's a wild man. He's got his head so full
of twisted ideas till he can't see straight.

Madelyn But I don't try telling him what to do.

George Perhaps you should; he acts like a boy.

Madelyn I've never wanted to live on a farm and be a farmer's wife,
and he'll make me a farmer's sister, mother, housekeeper, all the same.
I want to get away.

George Where to?

Madelyn Oh, I don't know, not even a real place probably. When I
was a little girl I used to dream of living in a castle; I'd be rich and
beautiful and have admirers queuing at the gates just for a glimpse of
me in my fine silks.

George Well, you're half there in the town here, there's a mass of men
at Jackson's would like to be me right now — sure we could charge
admission.

Madelyn And I'd have servants and livery and silver places set at mile-
long tables ... and my heels would dance on the floor like music as I
walked. I wanted to be so special. But I'm not special. Not really, I
can't do anything except raise disapproving eyebrows and bagfulls of
gossip.

George Ah but you do it well!

Madelyn Thank you ...

Pause; she drinks

George I don't know what to say. Do you not know you are special?

Madelyn Not in this town, not to Liam, Ma and Da gone, who's to be
special to?

George He's trying to protect you, it's his way ...

She smiles, knowing he is right. They take another sip of whiskey.
Madelyn picks up the cornet again

Madelyn I can't even play this — I'm about as special as the tremendous
trump I just made.

George I think your tremendous trump was very special — Madelyn
... Don't be ...

Madelyn Don't be what?

George Don't be put down by it all. You're a step above.

Madelyn Oh aye!

George Aye.

Pause; they have strayed away into an area they least expected

You can play it — I'm sure.

Madelyn How?

George Make a tiny jet of air, like if you make grass squeal on your lips out on the meadow.

Madelyn Give it me back then I'll try again.

George That's it, and fingers there and there, that's it, it's all in the lips, and the very tip of the tongue.

She tries again, this time a more recognizable note emerges. She is delighted, George claps his hands. As he describes which valves to press Madelyn haltingly plays the first four notes of "When the Saints Go Marching In"

That's the way! Now play that note again, then one and two, then one, then open again, now that'll be a tune of a sort ...

She plays a reasonable intro to "When the Saints Go Marching In"

There now, that's a note or two at least.

Madelyn My, but there's an art to this; it makes your lips ache like you've shut them in a mousetrap.

George They're sore red too, rose red.

Madelyn They are.

George They are, aye, they are.

Suddenly they both realize what is going to happen. George leans forward and kisses her, she kisses back. They both suddenly stop, straighten up and George takes a swig of whiskey

Madelyn That's a powerful strong note you're playing yourself, Constable.

George It's as true as any note I ever played.

Madelyn It is?

George It is — I swear it.

Pause. She tentatively takes his hand

Madelyn He says I'm not to see you, Constable.

George That's our business, and I think you should call me George, since we're now on friendly terms.

Madelyn And you always call me Madelyn please.

George Madelyn ...
Madelyn It's the name I prefer, Maddy always sounds like a put-me-down, halfway between mad and maddening.
George Madelyn. So it is. What will you do?
Madelyn Go back. It's my house as much as his.
George I'll walk you there.
Madelyn Will I be safe with you?
George I'm a policeman!

She still waits for an answer

Well yes of course you'll be safe with me. (*Taking the bottle and pouring another whiskey for them both*) Come, let's drink a toast to the friends we are now, then I'll take you home, and tomorrow I'll come round and talk with your man Liam and straighten him out. I've known him as long as it takes to know a man and he's a wild one all right, but not so bad he won't listen to reason, and if we're to be courting then he needs to know it.
Madelyn Courting — is that what it is?
George Courtin'. Oh God, so it is.
Madelyn What's the matter?
George Madelyn, I've had it in mind to kiss you a while now, but you know I'm to be sent back to Londonderry.
Madelyn And made a sergeant, that's grand.
George And made a sergeant.
Madelyn When will you go?
George It's next week. I've been meaning to say, I wasn't going to ... well ...
Madelyn Break my heart.
George Kiss you! I'm a coward.
Madelyn Well, it must be meant.
George Meant. Aye. I thought you were the one who controls your fate.
Madelyn I am, but I can't stop you going, I know that, I want you to go, except for wishing you back — you will come back?
George Aye!
Madelyn And now we'll see if a kiss makes a difference, won't we?
George Yes for sure.

George kisses her again, still sitting, but stops again

Madelyn Don't worry.
George No — no ... I can just feel things changing, it's a strange thing — new and strange.

Madelyn Could I try a bit more of the courting, Constable? Just to make sure of the taste of it.

She kisses him again. This time they stand and the cornet comes between them for a moment. George very deliberately puts it down on the chair. Madelyn kisses him very gently

    It's somewhere between marmalade and wine, this courting.
George Courtin' is that ? Or whiskey?
Madelyn Not sure ... Let me see ...

And another kiss. There is a sudden terrible hammering on the door, they ignore it. Music: An Orange marching band playing "King Billy's March" loudly drowning out the hammering

Fade to Black-out

ACT II

The cold croft room, at the wake. Autumn 1985

Music: John McCormack singing "Gardens Where the Praties Grow"

The Man is alone with the music. He pours another shot of whiskey, knocks it back, then pours another. The bottle is half empty

The music fades

The clock strikes three. Daniel comes in from the yard. He fetches his glass and sits at the table

Daniel Did you know her well? Before you went away ...?
The Man Not so well as I'd call it well. But we were passing friends. I knew her when she was a beauty, can you think of that? A real beauty, and there wouldn't be a man in Ireland, North or South of the border, would deny it. She'd make you stop and stare.
Daniel I never knew her young, but she knew me nothing else.

Silence

The Man You were lucky, to have her to yourself, lucky London Irish you see!
Daniel Lucky was I?
The Man Oh you were, for sure you were.

Pause

Daniel Why did she never marry, her being such a beauty?
The Man I don't know. She must've been asked, a round dozen times … She mustn't have wanted it, there's some it has no appeal for.
Daniel I heard a story there was a particular man, an Orangeman.

Music: "She Moved Through the Fair"

   Maddy is in the yard with a bucket of milk. She pauses and sits on the step of the house, in the sunlight

The Man You did? Well, yes, there must be stories, about Mad Madelyn Ingram.

Daniel She never spoke of him. (*He looks to the bedroom door*)

The Man goes to the yard doorway and stands looking out, over and beyond Maddy

The Man Did she not? No, no it does not surprise me — like I say she'd not be the marrying kind.
Daniel Did you know the man?
The Man I knew a man like that, many years ago, but not any more, no ... (*Half to himself*) There's another soul coming, surely, eh Madelyn? (*He sits by the harmonium, still looking out of the door*)
Daniel Mad Madelyn Ingram ...

Summer 1960

Maddy stands, comes through the door. She sees Young Daniel waiting for her

Maddy Lor's sake's, boy, look at you, what have you done to yourself?
Young Daniel It's nothing, a boy beat me.
Maddy Oh? He just beat you, without a reason?
Young Daniel He did, and I have the torn shirt to prove it, my mam will kill me next ...
Maddy She'll never kill you, Dan, not if you tell her what happened!
Young Daniel She'll kill me twice if I tell her that, then dance on my grave.
Maddy Tell me and we'll see.
Young Daniel You'll be angry too. You'll think I'm an eejit.
Maddy Just tell me. Why were you fighting him?
Young Daniel Because he called me names.
Maddy Well there's no hurt in names it's true, if you can close your ears ... Sure they've all called me Mad Maddy Ingram these twenty years, but I don't much care.
Young Daniel How do you not care?
Maddy Oh .... Because it keeps them away apart and leaves me in peace. They've decided who and what I am, and put me on the bar shelf to stare at. It's half true.
Young Daniel It's not true.
Maddy It's no matter whether it be true or not. What did he call you then, this grand insulter that got your knuckles so red?

A beat. The music fades

Well?

A beat

Young Daniel He said I was a Catholic bastard.

Silence, the insult hangs in the air. Maddy holds Daniel close

Maddy I see. And are you then?
Young Daniel Am I?
Maddy A Catholic bastard? Well let's be strict and straight and start at one end of it like a court of law. (*She takes the lace runner from the harmonium and places it over her hat like a comical judge's wig. She has a mischievous air*) All rise!

Young Daniel gets up, sheepishly

And in the dock with you!

He stands behind his chair, joining in the game

Will you swear on this holy — pail of milk, to tell the entire truth and no word of a lie.
Young Daniel Aye well, sort of ...
Maddy Are you, Daniel McKennan, a Catholic?
Young Daniel Yes, I ... well, I've never thought not ...
Maddy So you're born a Catholic and never thought to be anything else? Like a devil for instance, or a Protestant, or some other godless soul?
Young Daniel No, Miss.
Maddy And are you ashamed of that?
Young Daniel Of course not!
Maddy And secondly, and I want you to think most carefully about this before you answer the court: are you, strictly speaking — a bastard? Which is to say, were your mother and father married at all when you were conceived?
Young Daniel Conceived? Is that like consecrated?
Maddy Ah — we may be in for a rough ride here, ladies and gentlemen of the jury. Sit down, Daniel, will you not. Now, when a man (*she indicates the bucket*) and a woman (*she goes for the smaller buttermilk churn and puts it next to the bucket*) lie down together, and, well they ... well, a man and a woman are not entirely the same. (*She removes the lid of the buttermilk churn, then she makes the handle of the pail stand erect*) You know that, don't you now, Daniel? And when they ... well, sometimes they ... (*She tentatively pours the milk from the*

bucket into the buttermilk churn, then lowers the handle of the bucket and gives a little flourish. But then the whole exercise defeats her) Did your mother never mention this to you?

Pause

Young Daniel You mean feckin', dontcha!

Maddy There's no need to call a spade a shovel!

Young Daniel I'm sorry, Miss, but no they were not, my father was a rovin' man, my granda had a knife at his throat unless he did the proper thing by my mam — but he went away ... And besides, Ma, she was never so much of a beauty — but very willing — and you can see the bad of it in my own great mistake of a face.

Pause

Maddy Now none of that! So you are a bastard, and so he's right again this far-seeing lad that you beat to a pulp for the truth of his words. And here's the importance of it, and I want you to listen very carefully, Danny. Are you ashamed of being such a true and pure bastard?

Young Daniel My ma's not at all, so why should I? 'Cordin' to her it's a great thing to have as many kids as you can, to feed the spread of the Irish nation beyond, and increase the chances of making a good diamond bastard now and then!

Maddy Well, she's got an argument, albeit from the rovin' man's point of view that persuaded her to lie down. Anyway as regards your problem, the judgment is: that on both counts of the insult you are guilty — and I sentence you to hold your head up high and say, "Yes that's me, Daniel McKennan, a full-formed Catholic bastard. What of it?"

Young Daniel Well, I do yes ... I will.

Maddy Then it seems to me you should have shook this boy by the hand for his wisdom, not wrung him by the neck for his lies.

Young Daniel You're right, Miss, you are right, but he had a raw way of saying it ...

Music: "She Moved Through the Fair", very faint

Maddy It's the art of interpretation, Dan, you see it on the stage and in the pulpit as well as courts of law, that's what it is makes a compliment of a curse.

Young Daniel I'll tell him that, when I kick his arse again.

Maddy Good. So run along then, and tell your mother there's some good butter on the make if she's a mind to it.

*Maddy returns to the butter, taking the buttermilk can with her. She stops
at the mirror, as if caught by herself*

*The time reverts to 1985. The music fades as the clock strikes four.
Daniel becomes/is replaced by his older self again*

Daniel There's only us.
The Man Yes.

Pause

Daniel How do you remember her?
The Man How do I? There's a thing ...
Daniel What?
The Man I mean how can I? Can I? Memory does not afford me much
privilege — Miss Ingram. (*He considers*) No, I remember something
else, entirely.
Daniel I don't follow.
The Man Certain things. They take you back. Do you remember the
night they painted the statue of her majesty?
Daniel The Green Queen? I wasn't born. But I always heard about it; an
outrage, wasn't it? At the time.
The Man Aye! I had to clean it off, well most of it, and the devil of a
job it was.
Daniel You cleaned it?
The Man Yes, with turpentine and sandpaper. I was working for the
council, this and that ...
Daniel Oh aye? So you must have known her brother too, did he do it?
Like they all say?
The Man I knew him ... They still talked about that? These old boys?
Daniel It's a local legend; Michael Collins runs a poor second.

Music: "I Dreamt That I Dwelt in Marble Halls", like a siren call

Daniel There's only us. I'll take a look at her ...
The Man Yes.

Daniel goes into the bedroom

Spring 1935

*The Man and Maddy become/are replaced by George and Madelyn. If
doubling is in place George removes his coat, as Madelyn replaces his
jacket around her shoulders. They are both just as they were on the night*

of the kiss. They move together. George and Madelyn kiss as at the end of Act I

Madelyn It's somewhere between marmalade and wine, this courting.
George Courtin' is that? Or whiskey?
Madelyn Not sure ... Let me see ...

Another kiss. The terrible banging on the door again, the music fades. Madelyn and George do not stop kissing. The hammering persists

George (*eventually*) What the devil is that?
Madelyn It's the blood pounding in my head!

Another volley of banging. George goes to the window in the fourth wall and opens it

George (*shouting out to the street*) Who's there, what's this almighty racket will wake the deaf and the dead together?

It is Liam below (on the fore stage), he is drunk and furious, he staggers around the barracks

Liam (*off*) Is she in there? If she's there I'll kill you — you Protestant bastard!
George Oh you will?
Liam (*off*) I will, and all of you's all the way to Holyhead and then on ... Come on show your face.
George Go home, Liam, there's nothing for you here!
Liam (*off*) She's there!

Madelyn comes to the window

Madelyn Go home, Liam, there's no need for you to be here.
Liam (*off*) Do not leave me, Maddy, not for a Derry man!

The sound of Liam crashing into a dustbin outside, and falling over

(*Off*) Ah did you see, did you never see! He laid me low with a dustbin from behind! That's a British trick!

George shrugs his shoulders. He takes Madelyn in his arms again and they kiss

(*Off*) Will somebody rescue my sister, she's sufferin' in the hands of the law in there.

Madelyn exits. Liam enters

Music: an Orange marching band, very loud

The following day at the barracks (using the croft table and chair)

Liam is sitting at a bare table, looking furious. George is standing, trying to be the tough policeman

George So. Why should you do such a thing, where's the point in that?

Liam I did nothing. I took a drink, and I toasted the king.

George I've heard that a round dozen times this morning, Liam, from every lad in the town.

Liam So why keep askin'?

Pause

George A fine statue like that in the middle of town, and suddenly there's paint upon it! Is it a roamin' band of decorators I should be blaming?

Liam Aye well it wasn't me, I'd've been proud to, mind — and me no artist at all.

George So who did? Should I talk to every Fenian who had a drink last night, I'll be here till doomsday.

Liam Well who do you think? Who's going to paint the arse of Queen Victoria gloss green in the middle of the night? So it glows like a beacon in the morning sun. Well, it wasn't you for sure. So how about a Fenian? And then, Constable Park, does it matter which one?

George For Christ's sake, Liam, this is Enniskillen. If you want a fight — go to Spain, go get yourself murdered where there's no chance of blood on Irish streets!

Pause

Liam Have you touched her?

George Who, the queen?

Liam My sister, Madelyn my sister.

Pause. George considers his answer

George She was with me.

*Liam lurches at George, knocks his hat off, punches him in the stomach
and grabs him by the throat. The two of them stagger across the room
locked together. They both crash into the table. George gets Liam in an
arm lock*

Liam If you've touched her before you leave I'll kill you twice over,
you loyalist bastard.

George I've kissed her, and she me, if that's the touch you had in mind,
now lay your hands off me, what do you think I am?

Liam I should kill you.

*Another struggle. This time George gets the superior grip and he twists
Liam's arm behind him again and they both fall to their knees*

George Killing seems a harsh penalty for a tender kiss. I think she
enjoyed it!

Liam Now you're tauntin' me, Constable! Did you ever have a sister
kissed a man like yourself?

George You set yourself up, if you were Victoria's rear you'd be just as
green, like your jealous nature. For God's sake, Liam, can you not find
your sense of humour or should we send out a search party?

Liam My sense of humour! It's with your fat old queen's great arse!

George The poor woman's dead long before you desecrated her royal
— arse.

Liam Ha!

George And where's the harm in it, a little history, you can't write it
again ...

Liam You can! You can undo it. I'll swear no oath to a king beyond ...
a nation once again ... one Ireland!

George God, Liam, the North is British, it's as clear as the nose on
your face and, God help you, the green paint beneath your nails. That
there's a North and South of Ireland, it's a done deed, where's the
sense of this ...?

Liam stands, George gets his breath back

What's your problem with me? Is it that I'm a Protestant, or is it that
I'm a peeler?

Liam It's that you don't belong. I'm free. I'm leaving here, I'm going
home now, so should you, but further, go home, man, go home, go
home!

George I'm Irish, Liam. If I go Ireland goes with me ...

Liam goes to leave, but George will not give up

I'm going back to Londonderry, to be a sergeant. And I've a mind to ask your sweet sister to come too. And you'd be welcome yourself if you weren't such a piece of broken glass in a green field ... You'll do no good like this, Liam.

Liam Go to Derry — with you?

George Ah God, Liam, I think I'm in love with your sister.

Liam In love with her?

Pause

Have you asked her?

George I will ask her, and that's the end of it, and no more talk of the queen or green paint. It'll be her choice.

He offers his hand. Liam does not take it for a moment, then he does

Liam Her choice? Aye I'll drink to that.

Liam exits through the exterior door

George watches him go, then sets the table back where it was, takes a look around, and then follows Liam out

The Lights change to the croft room. The next day

Silence

Madelyn enters from the bedroom

Liam is asleep in the loft. Madelyn is bored. She goes to the stove, stirs the flame, looks out of the window, then she uncovers the harmonium and plays, increasingly furiously: "When the Saints Go Marching In"

(*Off*) Jesus will you stop that racket, I've got a head banging like a drum.

Liam enters with his jacket in his hand

Will you stop that, Maddy!

Madelyn continues playing

Maddy, I said will you stop that. For God's sake!

Madelyn slams down the lid of the harmonium. Silence. Liam puts his jacket on and sits at the table and wraps the jacket tightly around him: he is the worse for wear

Madelyn I'm leaving, Liam.

Liam You are? And where to now? Would you fancy another night in police barracks?

Madelyn That's more your level of accommodation. What would Mammy say if she knew?

Liam What? That you're being fingered by a peeler?

Madelyn (*stamping her foot*) I'm not, besides he's leaving, you know it.

Liam Well, that's convenient, so, eloping are you? Honest, Maddy, you've read too many romances: who do you think you are?

Madelyn I know who I am, Liam.

Liam And what's that supposed to mean?

Madelyn So who are you? My brother, is that the man? Or are you some black-haired hunter with a devil's soul? Which book's that from, eh Liam? Or are you just a drunk?

Liam You should not talk to me like that. I should slap you for that.

Pause. She faces him out

Madelyn Go on!

Pause. She turns away. He grabs her arm but the anger fades

Liam I — I care for you, Maddy.

Madelyn You do? I know, I'm sorry.

Liam I'm sorry too, it's a hard thing, to lose a sister.

Madelyn You're not losing me. You're right.

Liam Don't tease me, Maddy.

Madelyn Where am I going? I can't leave the farm, not now, there's a power of work to be done to turn it ...

Liam No, you will go, I can't stop that, but you must choose a man that will make you happy.

Madelyn You sound like Mother.

Liam Aye well, her ghost walks these ways awhile still, in mirrors and the like.

Madelyn I can't be happy if you're not.

Liam No. Well, that's the way of it.

Madelyn That's the way of it.

Madelyn walks into the bedroom

Liam becomes/is replaced by Daniel

The room of the wake returns. It is Autumn 1985

The Man returns from the yard

The Man You can see a bit of green there still, up on the queen's left
buttock. I looked there on my way through. It's a miraculous thing
how long paint sticks.
Daniel She never told me about that, or much about the brother.
The Man Did she not? Well there's a thing. Protectin' your Celtic
innocence like as not.
Daniel But this policeman, he did go away?

Pause

The Man Away. (*Pause*) Yes, away he went, so I believe. (*He looks
down the hill again; pause*) You know there's never another soul
coming, we'll have to carry her ourselves.
Daniel The coffin?
The Man If you will, London Irish, do you have any strength?
Daniel I never thought I'd do such a thing.
The Man She'll be light as a feather. I was thinking that awhile before
you came.
Daniel Yes.
The Man As I sat with her.
Daniel Yes. It was good of you.
The Man She was alone so long already.
Daniel Yes. 'Twas a shame.
The Man There's nothing of her ... (*He seems distressed*)
Daniel Are you all right ?
The Man It's the whiskey, always makes me see the gloom around, I'll
sit for a while. (*He sits*)
Daniel She died in her sleep. She would've known nothing.

Music underscore: "Carrickfergus"

*Madelyn appears in the yard. She has a letter and she waits in the
sunshine, seemingly reluctant to spoil the moment*

The Man No. She would've known nothing, nothing at all.

Pause

Daniel He must have died a while back, the brother.

The Man He did, I heard he did, he died after the war ... He couldn't fight, he wasn't fit, but he drank like a drain so he drowned for Ulster anyway.

Pause

Daniel I'll help you carry her.

Pause

The Man (*indicating the harmonium*) Can you play another tune on that thing? For her, to help her sleep?
Daniel Yes, yes I can I think. (*He opens the harmonium*) What would you like?
The Man Oh anything from the old times. Let's make her smile, eh?

Daniel gets the book of music from the shelf above the harmonium and looks through it. He plays "Carrickfergus", overlaying the underscore which fades

The old croft room returns. Spring 1935

The Man and Daniel become/are replaced by George and Daniel

Madelyn comes in with her letter. She goes to the centre of the room, by the table, and opens it. It contains a single rose and a letter on two sides of writing paper. As Madelyn reads, the young George speaks his letter, from his room in Derry, but to Madelyn as though he was with her

George Dear Madelyn, I hope that you are well and happy. I am back in Londonderry and have good lodgings at the address above. I am not much of a writer of letters but I hope that this will do for you, though it is plain and I am afraid to send it. I have one thing to say, which brings with it a thousand others. (*He moves close to her, almost touching her*) I love you with all my heart, Madelyn. Will you consent to be my wife? I know that I am never likely to be a wealthy man, but my prospects here are good, and we can live well, Madelyn. There is so much to do and see here, and talk about. (*He takes the rose, places it in her hand*) I would be the happiest man alive if we can share our lives together. I have spoken with Liam, I hope that he has told you. Please write soon and tell me your mind. If I hear nothing I will know it and will trouble you no more. With my love, George.

Madelyn puts the envelope and letter to her lips and smells the rose

During the following, George moves away and becomes/is replaced by The Man

Madelyn takes out pen and paper. She writes to George and she speaks

Madelyn Trouble me! Madelyn Park! 'Tis short and sweet. George — sure you're a timid man and bold all at once. I'll marry you. But I'll say to you, George, are you sure you want a girl like me? Are you sure you'd care for my tastes and wilful longings? You know me, George, and I know you. If you can see us arm in arm for all the time we have then I'll be yours for better or worse. But if you have a doubt at all you'd best disappear, and I'll carry my love in my own heart, for I have a love for you that I am frightened to spoil. So yes it is, a yes for all your thousand things, if you've the courage then so do I. I'll wait for you, George, till you come for me.

Madelyn finishes and seals the letter. Liam's playing ends with a flourish

Liam What do you think, Maddy, it's a good old tune? Sure I'll play it at the ceili come the summer and stir the crowd to tears.
Madelyn It's a fine tune.

He plays the final phrase again

Liam, will you be going down to the town later?
Liam Aye, I'm to meet the lads at Jackson's.
Madelyn Well will you post a letter for me at the office on the way, and not forget?

He stops playing. She drops all pretence of making light of the letter

Liam Aye
Madelyn Here it is ...

He looks at the address, unembarrassed about his curiosity

Liam (*reading the name*) "Sergeant George Park."
Madelyn Yes. That's your man.

Pause

Liam So what's the thing?

Pause, Liam knows

Sure you're not going to go and marry him are you?

Pause

Madelyn He asks me to.

Pause

Liam You are then, I can see it.
Madelyn I love him, and I would marry him for that.
Liam And you accept him, here in this letter?
Madelyn I know I have a duty to you, Liam, and to the farm, I cannot just walk away from that — not without ... But you will not leave — you will not … Mammy said to make sure you were strong, before I married.
Liam I'm strong, Maddy.
Madelyn There's a mountain of work here, Liam, but I want to see you happy — and I know you rarely are — and it's myself that's your misery half the time ... Agh will you help me, Liam?
Liam But you say yes?

Pause, she searches his eyes for some sign of acceptance

Madelyn You said I must choose a man will make me happy.
Liam I know I said it ...
Madelyn So don't you believe it? He told me he spoke with you, Liam, that you'd accept my choice.
Liam So you've made up your mind, Maddy?
Madelyn Yes. Give me your blessing, Liam?

Liam says nothing

You don't have to say a thing to me about it, but if you take it to the post ... I will know that you love me and want me happy, and yourself as well ...
Liam You want me to post it?
Madelyn Yes.
Liam Why can't you post it yourself?
Madelyn Because I want your blessing.

Pause, he meets her gaze

Liam I'll take it ...
Madelyn You will!
Liam I'll take it now. I promise.

He gets his cap, puts it on, puts the letter in his pocket. As he is about to go Madelyn holds him close. He is struggling with himself, unable to either go or stay

Madelyn There'll be someone for you, Liam; I'll make friends up there, and you'll have the pick of them like a fine bunch of roses.
Liam Aye, maybe. Yes ... So you'll come see your brother in Fermanagh now and then, will you now — when you're a fine lady and the law in skirts itself in Derry?
Madelyn Oh Liam ... I'm getting married ...

Liam leaves, taking the letter with him

Music: "Irish Mist" by Boolavogue, plays softly

Madelyn is left in the room

The Man stands in the bedroom doorway, watching her as if in memory. In fact he is talking to her as he surely was before Daniel arrived at the start, so time slips between 1935 and 1985 during the following sequence

Madelyn sits at the table, joyfully, it is her happiness, her moment

The clock strikes five. The Man is in the bedroom doorway

The Man You lying there — and you were such a beauty, God if there wasn't a man wouldn't've died for you. And that kiss of yours. 'Twas like the warm dew. Madelyn. On those cold lips ...

Madelyn begins to busy herself around the room, tidying, killing time

Madelyn No, he's busy, silly girl, it's a new job and all. Be patient. There's much to be sorted and fixed and he'll be in a fierce rush to make it right.
The Man Why do we do that, make a choice one day, one minute in one day, one second that sends the rest of our time ticking to a different beat.
Madelyn Should I write again?
The Man I should have written again. But I left it alone.

Madelyn goes into the bedroom

Another day. Morning

Liam (*off, from the yard*) Maddy! Maddy! Have you fed the sow?
Madelyn (*off, from the bedroom*) There's a bucket in the yard!
Liam (*off, from the yard*) Oh for God's sake, Maddy!

Another day. Midday

   Madelyn comes in from the bedroom

Madelyn (*cleaning the harmonium*) What will our children look like? If
they had the worst of us both they'd be cursed, the poor souls. But 'tis
their fate to be born as nature will have them, beauty's within, that's
what Mother said.

Madelyn stares out of the window

The Man Here's the scar of a wound that will always be tender. I'm all
scar; there's no flesh not burned.

Another day. Early evening. Madelyn stares at the clock

Madelyn That clock. Have you wound the clock, Liam, I'm sure it's
stopped.

   Liam comes out of the bedroom. He is on his way out

Liam Well if it's stopped I haven't wound it!
The Man And the weeks into brittle months, a shell of time to shelter
in.
Madelyn Sure he'd reply if he meant what he said.
Liam Sure he'll reply, give him a chance. Have you seen my hat?
Madelyn It's in your pocket.

   Liam leaves

Another day. The music slowly fades. Late evening

The Man It was a tender kiss, that's all.
Madelyn I'll wait for you, George, until you come for me.
The Man I should have come here.
Madelyn He would have come here.
The Man I was so afraid.
Madelyn Don't worry.
The Man Silence.

The music is gone

Madelyn Not a word.
The Man Silence.
Madelyn Not a word.
The Man Silence.

The Man goes into the bedroom, taking the bottle of whiskey with him

Spring, 1935. A bright, plain day

Madelyn fetches the farm accounts ledger. She examines the bills she finds tucked between the pages; there are many unpaid

Liam walks into the yard and sees her through the door

Overwhelmed, Madelyn furiously sweeps the bills on to the floor, just as Liam comes in, the worse for wear. There are papers spilled everywhere. Maddy starts to pick them up, tears in her eyes

Liam Maddy — what ails ye?
Madelyn Leave me. I'm fine, I slipped.
Liam Sure you were aimin' for the fire with them bills? Have another go ... (*He drunkenly aims at the fire with a bill*)
Madelyn Don't, Liam, go away, I'll sort this.
Liam I'll help.
Madelyn (*shouting*) Leave it be, Liam! I'll do it!
Liam Maddy, you've the temper of a mongrel hound!
Madelyn Then be warned!
Liam Ah 'tis me, Maddy. 'Tis your own brother. What is it?

Madelyn again stoops to pick up the papers and he tries to help. He puts some bills and sale dockets on the table

Madelyn No, they need some order, they're all higgledy, they're all ... Put them in separate piles, paid and not. Oh, they're all muddled, muddled ...

Madelyn is in a restrained fury. Liam tries to hold her and she fights him off

Liam Come on now, Maddy, what is it? There now, you're safe.
Madelyn No, I'm not, not safe.

Liam You are. What's to worry about? Them bills is nothing, we'll pay;
it's a bad time that's all, it's the same the world over ...
Madelyn I'm in a panic.
Liam I know. But don't. Don't ... It's all right, come on now sit down
— we'll sort these out. (*He tries to sort out the bills himself*)

After a while she slams the ledger shut again

Madelyn There's nothing come.
Liam I know.
Madelyn He's not writ ...
Liam No.
Madelyn I don't know what to do.
Liam Shall I go there? Tell him my mind?
Madelyn No ... no.
Liam I've a mind to brain him for wounding you so.
Madelyn No, Liam ...
Liam Time then, time's all there is.
Madelyn Oh Liam, I'm sorry.
Liam Nothing to be sorry about.
Madelyn I'm sorry, I'm sorry.

*Liam holds her. He begins to sing gently "Gardens Where the Praties
Grow". It calms her. Liam goes to the harmonium and begins to pick out
the tune. Madelyn softly sings as she resignedly puts the ledger back on
the shelf. She sits at the window in the fourth wall. She is close to tears*

The cold room returns. Autumn 1985

> *The Man is there, in the bedroom doorway. He is holding the nearly-
> empty whiskey bottle*

Liam becomes/is replaced by Daniel. The music stops

*During the following, Madelyn, still sitting at the window, becomes/is
replaced by Maddy. If doubling is in place Madelyn becomes older in
a physical sense as she watches: she stoops and acquires the sunken
appearance of the older woman, though still in the younger Madelyn's
dress*

The Man It's a strange thing to do, I'm thinking, to walk away out of
one life and into another ...
Daniel Meaning?

The Man You, and your living over there, and your memories and Ma still in Fermanagh ...

Daniel I don't think about it, I'll probably live here again.

The Man Buy a farm will you? With your London money, and live the life of a countryman?

Daniel Why do you dislike me?

The Man I don't. Not in the least. Don't mind me. I probably envy you.

Daniel Envy?

The Man I envy your freedom. You've walked away from it all. Catholic, Protestant, God does it matter a bollocks to you? I'd be surprised if you give it a thought.

Daniel I'm still Irish. But the world moves on.

The Man No, the world stays here and waits. You're some kind of European, with your Celtic burr — and your fancy feckin' coat! Are you a married man, London Irish?

Daniel No.

The Man Jesus, you're as free as a falling angel, fallen from your Irish heaven, that you thought was hell, and you're still falling, and you'll never be anywhere. You're an exile, man, you've walked out on Ireland and she won't have you back, not never no how.

Daniel What makes you different?

The Man Me. I'm an Ulster man. I'm an Orangeman. I have an identity. I didn't give up on my country. I fought for it, I served.

Daniel No. You're an exile too. You fell. You're neither Irish nor English. You're just the man with the big stick in between, Royal Ulster Constabulary, was it? Was that your life?

The Man Aye it was! And proud of it!

Daniel Are you a married man — (*with cruel emphasis*) Constable George Park? Or did you never "walk out on that" either?

Silence. The Man walks to the yard door and looks through. He accepts his name

You must have a brood of rosy grandchildren all banging drums in Derry since you're so proud.

The Man I have not, there's never been ...

Daniel Then why — George Park — why?

Pause

The Man She never accepted ...

Pause

Daniel What possessed you to stay quiet, man. Why not come back?
The Man She did not want me.
Daniel Did you love her!

Pause. The Man turns to Daniel. Almost in fury he approaches him, a threat for a moment

The Man She has been the meaning of love to me ...

Slowly he retreats to the door

1963

Maddy, still at the window, is now an older woman, the oldest we have yet seen her

Maddy (*shouting into the loft bedroom, putting on her apron*) Will you wind the clock, it's stopped. I can hear the clock ticking but the clock's stopped. (*She looks in the mirror*) Ah Mammy, and where have you been ... Stop time for me, will you? Put your finger on the hands of fate and stop the wee things going round ... In fact let's turn it back and start again, sure I've a mind to change it all ...

Young Daniel is in the doorway, now about sixteen

Young Daniel Miss Ingram?
Maddy Madelyn, that's the name I love ...
Young Daniel Madelyn.

She turns from the mirror, recognizes him. He has not visited for a while and has become a young man. She collects herself, hardens a little

Maddy You've grown.
Young Daniel I have.
Maddy You'll be going away?
Young Daniel When the time comes.
Maddy Remember your promise, boy?
Young Daniel I remember.
Maddy Do you still like the music?
Young Daniel I do. I play piano. They say I'm good, shall I show you ...? (*He indicates the harmonium*)
Maddy No, no, don't play that. Sure you'll play like an angel, but not on that ... No, no ... (*She takes the key to the clock from the shelf and puts it on the table*) Will you wind the clock, Daniel, it's stopped.

Young Daniel I will.

Maddy Twelve turns to the right. My brother used to do it. I can never be bothered; the time passes quick all the same, if the clock ticks or not.

Young Daniel That's true enough.

Maddy Imagine if it didn't? There'd not be a single clock or watch tickin' in the whole of Ireland, except in the pockets of suicides and reckless souls who'd never heard of wrinkles and death and worms in the ground.

Young Daniel That's a wild idea.

Maddy My brother was a terrible one for windin' that clock.

Young Daniel When did he die?

Pause. She searches his face for the time

Maddy Yesterday. Sixteen years ago. The clock will know. I was out. I'd gone to Enniskillen. For his insulin I'd collect on a Thursday, and see the market, and call at Kellands. He was there where you stand, and Jackson's dog stone dead in the yard, its neck clean broke, and a cold sweat on Liam would drown a man.

Young Daniel That was the dog that Marco killed.

Maddy Who told you that?

Young Daniel You did.

Maddy 'Twas what I told Jackson. Oh did you ever hear of a goose could kill a hound? It's a tale for a child ... But the old fool fell for it. My brother hated the mongrel, and he hated Jackson from long back, and the dog would come sniffin' round the chickens and eating the poor scraps. Liam had a temper would shock a maniac, and he was drunk, so that day he killed the dog, broke its neck with a shovel — Liam killed that dog stone dead. And Marco the old goose was safe there with him too. But he was shaken hard by what he'd done. He was sitting there with his bottle but with no good in it ... I got him up the stair but he fainted clean away, and he was cold like stone. Well I went for the doctor, he came with his needle. The diabetes come, like Daddy, and 'twas the doctor asked about the dog and so I told him the goose had done it, it seemed too cruel a thing for a man to do, and Liam, Liam was still breathing, but the doctor could not bring him back, he'd fallen too deep ...

A silence

Have you wound the clock, Daniel?

Young Daniel No, no, I'll do it.

Maddy Would you like his guitar? He'll never play it now.
Young Daniel Are you sure? I mean aye, I'd love it.
Maddy Wind the clock. 'Tis good for five days. That will be five more
spent. I think I've a great wealth of days to spend, and 'tis a good fast
tick ... (*Going towards the bedroom, she passes the guitar*) There it
is.

Maddy goes into the bedroom

*The older Daniel replaces the key on the shelf, picks up the guitar case,
takes out the guitar and plays "I Dreamt that I Dwelt in Marble Halls",
then, as the tune changes to a rough and ready "Garden Where the
Praties Grow" he becomes/is replaced by Liam. He is drunk*

Spring, 1938

> *The younger Madelyn comes out of the bedroom, the light has gone
> from her, there is some of old Maddy's hardness*

Madelyn Liam? Liam, did you call?. Did you ask? Liam?
Liam The post? Sure I called. I asked ...
Madelyn Well?
Liam Maddy it's been three years ...
Madelyn I know. To the day.
Liam And no word, Maddy. What do you expect? He's gone. He'll not
come back.
Madelyn I'll never believe that.
Liam Maddy, you're throwing away your life.
Madelyn It's mine to throw, so far as I like!
Liam Maddy, accept it. He will never come for you. His letter was not
meant, he's met some Derry girl and had two fat little RUC coppers by
now — bangin' their drums ...
Madelyn Shut up!
Liam If he'd loved you enough he'd have written again ...
Madelyn Shut up! Shut up!!

*Liam fetches a bottle and pours a glass. He sits at the table. Madelyn
leans over the table and she pulls the bottle from him*

> It's a hard thing for a woman to be forgotten. I've had an ache so long
> now that it's part of me, and it's part of you and this house too. It's
> changed me. Do you understand?

Liam I liked the way you were before.

Madelyn No you didn't, Liam.

Pause

Liam Forgotten are you — aye well and who else? Eh Maddy? Am I forgotten? Am I? God you're so full of sorrows I'm drowning here, Maddy, will you not pull me out? Will you not?

Pause

Why do you want him? And not me ...

Pause

Well here's to you, Maddy, and your aching heart!

Madelyn angrily pushes the bottle over the table to Liam so that he has to catch it. He drinks, then slaps the cork back into it

Liam takes his bottle and glass away. He becomes/is replaced by the Young Daniel

Music plays softly: "I Dreamt that I Dwelt in Marble Halls"

Time slips between 1955, 1965 and 1985

Young Daniel Miss Ingram, are you all right? I heard your singing.

The Man returns. He has the nearly-empty whiskey bottle and drains the last of the bottle into his glass

The Man She had a voice could charm the angels ... all those falling Irish angels, all listening with their eyes smiling.
Daniel (*as an adult*) Are the angels all Irish?
The Man Of course, how else could heaven be built on earth, but with Irish angels — and McAlpine cranes?

Summer, 1965. Young Daniel is with Maddy. His last visit

Young Daniel And are you keeping well, Miss Ingram? I heard you had a chill.
Maddy I'm well, Daniel, thank you, strong as a sow, though sweeter smellin'. And what's new or strange today?

Young Daniel There's a new baby at the Hendricks house, a boy, to be called Connor, like his da.

Maddy Bless that house for a new life's a fine thing.

Young Daniel And every finger and toe to perfection. My ma says 'tis a miracle when you see the parents.

Maddy Aye well ... But you, Dan, you're teasin' me — what's the news, did you get it?

Young Daniel Well ...

Maddy Tell me, boy!

Young Daniel I got it!

Maddy I knew it!

Young Daniel I'll be in London in three months, and a fine student of the musical arts!

Maddy I knew it! I knew it by the sound of your boots on the stones, you were floating, boy, like an angel.

Young Daniel I can't believe it. I mean I can believe it, but not that they'd want me. And the scholarship and all!

Maddy guides him to the doorway as if to show him the way. She turns him there, a small circle like a dance, and continues herself, as far as the step, as though Daniel is now heading down the lane

Maddy Ride the wind, boy, that blows you away, it's a sweet breath, 'tis a melody ... (*During the following, she moves to the table with her writing box and takes out the letter, now read a thousand times, and the rose, dried and black*)

Autumn, 1985. The Lights dim. The older Daniel is with George. The music fades

Daniel Why the devil did you never come back?

Pause. The Man is at a loss

   Why?

The Man Pride. The scorn of a woman. I was afraid, and time passed.

Daniel You should have known her better.

The Man She did not want me, can you not feel that? It's a twisting knife.

Daniel So you thought you were banished.

The Man I was lost. I was not so strong — I was a coward.

Daniel And the man on foot she didn't want, and the man on horseback passed her by ...

The Man What do you mean?
Daniel You need not have been lost.
The Man Why not, oh God, lad, you've not felt it.
Daniel No. I've not felt it. But there's more, there's more to the story of the constable.

1965. The Lights pick out Maddy at the table with her writing box

Maddy So tell me, George, what's new or strange today?

Back in 1985

The Man So tell me!
Daniel It involves the brother, Liam.
The Man He was a wild dog.
Daniel He loved her too, he was a brother.
The Man 'Tis another love.
Daniel A possession, a blood bond.
The Man So tell me. Tell me — the gossip.

Pause

Tell me, boy!
Daniel You wrote to Madelyn and asked her to reply ...
The Man I did.
Daniel And you said?
The Man I told her I loved her, and I asked her to marry me ...

Maddy is still with the letter, in the past, as The Man and Daniel speak

Maddy "Madelyn Park", 'tis short and sweet, I'll wait for you, George, till you come for me ...

1985

Daniel And you never had a reply?
The Man She never replied, never a word.

Daniel becomes/is replaced by Liam in Maddy's memory as he was in 1935; Maddy remains old

Liam Sure you're not going to go and marry him, are you?
Madelyn He asks me to.
Liam You are then, I can see it.

Madelyn I love him, and I will marry him for that.
Liam And you accept him, in this letter?
Madelyn I want you to post it, Liam. You don't have to say a thing to me about it, but if you take it to the post — I will know that you love me and want me happy, and yourself as well.

Pause. Liam becomes/is replaced by Daniel once more

The Man What are you telling me, boy? What do you know?
Daniel They said that she fell in love with a handsome policeman in the local barracks, and he with her. He was promoted to sergeant and transferred to another part of the country. He had written to her, asking her to marry him and she had replied, saying she would ——
The Man No 'tis not true — there was no reply!
Daniel She had given the letter to her brother to post, but he had never done it, he had torn it up and thrown it over the bridge into the river. Wanted a housekeeper, do you see?

The Man sits. He is in great pain. Pause

The Man Who told you this?
Daniel My mother told me, my father told her, drunk one night — before he died.
The Man Liam ...

Daniel nods

Daniel My father Liam. So I never knew him, only the story. You'd have heard it yourself — if you'd set a foot in the place.
The Man She replied ...
Daniel Yes, he tore it up, and her words of love floated away on the brown water, and disappeared forever out there — in the depths of Lough Erne.

Pause

The Man Madelyn!

Silence. The clock strikes six

As the clock strikes Maddy stands, loosens her hair and sheds her old housecoat. She becomes the young Madelyn again. The Man sits in despair at her side

Did she know — God help me, Dan? Did she ever know?

Pause

Daniel When I heard her sing, that first time, when she was old, she was singing to you ... Wasn't she? To the ashes in the empty hearth, and you ...

Pause

The Man Yes ... Thank you, thank you, Daniel.

Silence, they meet each other's gaze

Daniel It's time. (*He puts his coat back on*) We should take her from this place.

Daniel exits into the bedroom

Pause

Madelyn sings again, and this time to The Man. George has always been there, her love for all her life, her fantasy. As she sings, Madelyn takes the rose and puts it in The Man's buttonhole, as if they were going to a wedding. The Man looks up into her face, as though she were really there. The old man, and the young woman. Together across time. Madelyn sings, unaccompanied. As she sings, the Lights fade to catch only the two former lovers

Madelyn   I had riches too great to count, could boast
                              Of a high ancestral name,
                              But I also dreamt which pleased me most
                              That you loved me still the same
                              That you loved me,
                              You loved me still the same
                              That you loved me,
                              You loved me still the same.

Slow fade to Black-out

THE END

Calls accompanied by music: "I Dreamt that I Dwelt in Marble Halls"

FURNITURE AND PROPERTY LIST

ACT I

On stage: Portable pedal harmonium with a lace runner. *Covering it*: dust cloth. *Above it*: shelf with book of music and ledger of farm accounts containing bills and sales dockets
Piano stool
Crucifix on upstage wall
Belfast sink. *In it*: jug of water. *Above it*: single tap. *Above it*: shelf with 4 glasses, 3 cups and saucers
Shelves UR. *On them*: pots, pans, plates, 4 glasses, 3 cups and saucers, teapot, tray, **Madelyn**'s writing box containing writing paper, envelopes and pen, letter comprising 2 sheets, dried and blackened rose
Cottage table. *On it*: key to clock
2 wooden dining chairs with faded seat covers
Milking stool
Pot stove. *On it*: kettle. *Beside it*: pile of peat or logs, poker, dust-pan and brush
Mirror on wall UL
Clothes hooks on wall UL. *On one*: man's cap
Buttermilk churn
Goose egg wrapped in straw in a milk can (for **Daniel**)

Off stage: Bunch of three white roses, guitar in battered old guitar case (**Daniel**)
Three red roses in a vase (**Maddy**)
Bicycle with bell (**George**)
Small, wrapped bundle containing corked bottle of poteen (**Liam**)
Cornet (**George**)

Personal: **The Man**: opened bottle of whiskey in coat pocket
Liam: two bills in pocket

ACT II

Strike: Tea things from table

Check: Half-empty whiskey bottle and two glasses on the table

Re-set: Furniture to original positions

Set: Bottle of whiskey on shelf

Check: Half-empty whiskey bottle and two glasses on the table

Off stage: Bucket of milk (**Maddy**)
Envelope containing two sheets of writing paper and rose (**Madelyn**)
Jacket (**Liam**)

LIGHTING PLOT

ACT I

To open: Dull, cold interior on croft room with autumn exterior on croft step/yard

Cue 1   **Daniel**: "Is there a soul in the house?"   (Page 4)
           Slowly bring up brighter, warm effect for interior with
              summer sunshine exterior on croft step/yard

Cue 2   **Daniel** becomes his older self, **The Man** returns   (Page 6)
           Revert to dull, cold interior with autumn exterior on
              croft step/yard

Cue 3   **Maddy** turns to the harmonium   (Page 8)
           Gradually bring up brighter, warm effect for interior with
              summer sunshine exterior on croft step/yard

Cue 4   **The Man** strolls out into the yard   (Page 11)
           Change to indicate different time, with spring exterior
              on croft step/yard

Cue 5   **Madelyn** leaves, exasperated   (Page 16)
           Revert to dull, cold interior with autumn exterior on
              croft step/yard

Cue 6   As **Madelyn** enters   (Page 16)
           Start slow change to lighting for hoolie room

Cue 7   **George** and **Madelyn** move outside   (Page 20)
           Crossfade to exterior night effect

Cue 8   **George and Madelyn** exit   (Page 22)
           Crossfade to night interior on croft room; very
              gradually bring up dawn on room and croft step/yard

Cue 9   **Madelyn** moves to the window   (Page 22)
           Warm daylight on room and croft step/yard

Cue 10   Noise of **George** practising the cornet   (Page 29)
           Crossfade to evening effect on barrack room area

66   I Dreamt I Dwelt in Marble Halls

Cue 11   Orange marching band playing "King Billy's March"   (Page 35)
               Fade to black-out

ACT II

To open: Dull, cold interior on croft room with autumn exterior on croft step/
           yard

Cue 12   **Daniel**: "… an Orangeman."   (Page 36)
               Bring up sunlight on croft step/yard

Cue 13   **Daniel**: "Mad Madelyn Ingram …"   (Page 37)
               *Crossfade to warm effect on interior, sunlight on croft
               step/yard*

Cue 14   **Maddy** stops at the mirror   (Page 40)
               *Revert to dull, cold interior on croft room with
               autumn exterior on croft step/yard*

Cue 15   **Daniel**: "Yes."   (Page 40)
               *Crossfade to warm effect on interior, spring sunshine
               on croft step/yard*

Cue 16   **Liam**: (off) "… of the law in there."   (Page 41)
               Crossfade to interior of barrack room area

Cue 17   **George** follows **Liam** out   (Page 44)
               *Crossfade to warm effect on interior, spring sunshine
               on croft step/yard*

Cue 18   **Madelyn**: "That's the way of it."   (Page 45)
               *Crossfade to dull, cold interior on croft room with
               autumn exterior on croft step/yard*

Cue 19   **Daniel**: "She would've known nothing."   (Page 46)
               Bring up spring sunshine on croft step/yard

Cue 20   As **Daniel** plays the harmonium   (Page 47)
               *Change to warm interior on room with spring sunshine
               on croft step/yard*

Cue 21   **Madelyn** goes into the bedroom   (Page 50)
               Subtle change to indicate another morning

Cue 22   **Liam** (off) "Oh, for God's sake, Maddy!"   (Page 51)
               Subtle change to indicate another midday

EFFECTS PLOT

Please read the notice on page vii concerning the use of music.

ACT I

Cue 1   To open   (Page 1)
                 Music: James Galway's recording of intro to "I Dreamt
                 that I Dwelt in Marble Halls", fade as scene starts

Cue 2   **Daniel**: "Is there a soul in the house?" Pause   (Page 1)
                 Ticking clock (heard throughout); clock strikes twelve

Cue 3   **The Man**: "… the name I knew her by …" Pause   (Page 3)
                 Music underscore: James Galway's recording of intro to
                 "She Moved Through the Fair"; continue

Cue 4   **The Man**: "I'm sorry to hear her trouble."   (Page 4)
                 Music increases in volume; continue

Cue 5   As the scene changes to 1955   (Page 4)
                 Steam from kettle on stove

Cue 6   **Daniel**: "… what little there was of her …"   (Page 5)
                 Fade music

Cue 7   **Maddy**: "Honk honk!   (Page 6)
                 Music underscore: James Galway's recording of intro to
                 "She Moved Through the Fair"; continue

Cue 8   **Maddy**: "I'll put this safe away."   (Page 6)
                 Clock strikes one

Cue 9   **Maddy** takes the egg to the pantry   (Page 6)
                 Fade music

Cue 10   **The Man**: "… a big mouth full of flappin' tongues."   (Page 7)
                 Music: James Galway's recording of intro to "I Dreamt
                 that I Dwelt in Marble Halls"; continue

Cue 11   **The Man** begins to play the harmonium   (Page 9)
                 Fade music

Cue 12	**Maddy**: " … John McCormack or Gigli?" *Music underscore: James Galway's recording of intro to* *"She Moved Through the Fair"; continue*	(Page 11)
Cue 13	**The Man** strolls out into the yard *Music increases in volume; continue*	(Page 12)
Cue 14	Bicycle bell rings *Fade music*	(Page 12)
Cue 15	**Madelyn** leaves, exasperated *Clock strikes twice*	(Page 16)
Cue 16	**Daniel**: "I will, thanks." *Music underscore: last few bars of "Finnea Lassies"*	(Page 17)
Cue 17	**The Man**: " … never to have it." *Music swells; hoolie room noise as script pages 17-19*	(Page 17)
Cue 18	**Liam**: " … with only two left feet!" *Band begin to play "Kitty's Rambles", followed by* *"Finnea Lassies"*	(Page 20)
Cue 19	**George** and **Madelyn** move outside *Band music muted*	(Page 20)
Cue 20	**George**: "'Twill take a great effort." *Band music grows louder*	(Page 22)
Cue 21	**Madelyn** is away *Band music and hoolie noise intensifies then fades*	(Page 22)
Cue 22	**Liam**: "I'm asking." **Madelyn** is furious *Sound of rain on tin roof*	(Page 28)
Cue 23	**Liam**: "Maddy! Don't take on …" *Rain effect intensifies*	(Page 29)
Cue 24	**Liam** smiles to himself and drinks *Rain effect intensifies further*	(Page 29)

Cue 25	**Madleyn**: "Let me see …" **George** and **Madelyn** kiss
	 Hammering on door; music: an Orange marching band
	   playing "King Billy's March", loudly drowning out
	   the hammering
		(Page 35)

ACT II

Cue 26   To open   (Page 36)
              Music: John McCormack singing "Garden Where the
              Praties Grow"

Cue 27   **The Man** pours a second shot of whiskey   (Page 36)
              Music fades, clock strikes three

Cue 28   **Daniel**: "… an Orangeman."   (Page 36)
              Music: "She Moved Through the Fair"

Cue 29   **Maddy**: "… your knuckles so red?" A beat   (Page 37)
              Music fades

Cue 30   **Daniel**: "… a raw way of saying it …"   (Page 39)
              Music: "She Moved Through the Fair" plays very faintly

Cue 31   **Maddy** stops at the mirror   (Page 40)
              Music fades; clock strikes four

Cue 32   **Daniel**: " … runs a poor second."   (Page 40)
              Music: "I Dreamt that I Dwelt in Marble Halls"

Cue 33   **Madelyn**: "Let me see …"   (Page 41)
              Hammering on door; music fades; hammering

Cue 34   **Madelyn**: "… pounding in my head!"   (Page 41)
              Volley of banging

Cue 35   **Liam**: (off) "… not for a Derry man!"   (Page 41)
              *Sound of **Liam** crashing into dustbin outside and*
              *   falling over*

Cue 36   **Liam**: (off) "… of the law in there."   (Page 41)
              Music: very loud Orange marching band

Cue 37   **Daniel**: "She would've known nothing."   (Page 46)
              Music underscore: "Carrickfergus"

Cue 38   **Daniel** starts to play "Carrickfergus"   (Page 47)
              Fade music underscore

Cue 39   **Liam** leaves, taking the letter with him   (Page 50)
              Music: "Irish Mist" by Boolavogue, plays softly

Cue 40   **Madelyn** sits at the table   (Page 50)
              Clock strikes five

Cue 41	**Liam** leaves *Music starts to fade slowly*	(Page 51)
Cue 42	**The Man**: "Silence." *Cut music*	(Page 51)
Cue 43	**Liam** becomes the young **Daniel** *Music softly: "I Dreamt that I Dwelt in Marble Halls"*	(Page 58)
Cue 44	**Maddy**: "… 'tis a melody …" *Music fades*	(Page 59)
Cue 45	**The Man**: "Madelyn!" Pause *Clock strikes six*	(Page 61)
Cue 46	For curtain calls *Music: "I Dreamt that I Dwelt in Marble Halls"*	(Page 62)